More Luck of a Lancaster

More Luck of a Lancaster

109 Operations, 315 Crew, 101 Killed in Action

Gordon Thorburn

Pen & Sword
AVIATION

First published in Great Britain in 2017 by
Pen & Sword Aviation
an imprint of
Pen & Sword Books Ltd
47 Church Street
Barnsley
South Yorkshire
S70 2AS

Copyright © Gordon Thorburn 2017

ISBN 978 1 47389 766 3

Typeset in Ehrhardt by
Mac Style Ltd, Bridlington, East Yorkshire
Printed and bound in Malta by Gutenberg Press Ltd.

Pen & Sword Books Ltd incorporates the imprints of Pen & Sword
Archaeology, Atlas, Aviation, Battleground, Discovery, Family
History, History, Maritime, Military, Naval, Politics, Railways,
Select, Transport, True Crime, and Fiction, Frontline Books, Leo
Cooper, Praetorian Press, Seaforth Publishing and Wharncliffe.

For a complete list of Pen & Sword titles please contact
PEN & SWORD BOOKS LIMITED
47 Church Street, Barnsley, South Yorkshire, S70 2AS, England
E-mail: enquiries@pen-and-sword.co.uk
Website: www.pen-and-sword.co.uk

Contents

Preface:
Captain's Luck

Sergeant Norman Wells was a rear gunner with No. 9 Squadron in 1943/44 and one of the lucky men who got to the end of their tours of thirty operations.

'I don't know what made a brilliant pilot. We thought our skipper Phil Plowright was brilliant. Possibly they all were, or most of them, but most of them weren't lucky.

'When we were in L, our own aircraft, we were hit and came home on three engines, then we went on leave and she went down with another crew. We went to Marseille in B, got a shell in the tail, came home, gave her back to her former owner, very experienced pilot, and down he went with the Group Captain on board, and we were there on the same op, just like them, in among it.

'We were nominated PFF (Pathfinder Force) Supporter for Stuttgart, which is muggins who flies in front of the pathfinders to draw the fire so they can drop their TIs (Target Indicators) undisturbed. After doing that, you have to go around and come in again to bomb. We were in J-Johnny, never got a mark on that one, yet Backwell–Smith, a squadron leader, top man, FTR (failed to return). Nürnberg, that dreadful, dreadful night, we never got shot at but we damned nearly got rammed by another Lanc heading for the same cloud as we were. He was so close we could hear his engines as well as our own. I went to Berlin seven times, Frankfurt three times. Goodness knows how many went down on those trips.*

'Another time, we were flying almost wingtip to wingtip with this Lanc, straight and level on our bombing runs, and he had a flak shell burst behind him at the perfect height, then another in front, and the third hit him right amidships and he just went up in a cloud of bits. You were not supposed to deviate from your run in any circumstance. If you did, it would show on your photograph, it would be at a funny angle, and the skipper would be up before the CO. So that chap didn't deviate and they got the chop. He was close enough, so even in the dark I could have taken his squadron letters, if I'd known that was going to happen. Everyone was supposed to report any losses he saw, give what information he could to the navigator. Usually it was no more than aircraft going down so many yards to starboard. I could have been really precise on that one.'

SECRET: No. 9 Squadron Combat Report

Date: 20 December 1943. Time: 19.45. Height: 20,000 ft. Target: Frankfurt. Lancaster: G. Captain: P/O Glover

Shortly before approaching the target the bomber was swept by cannon and machine-gun fire, which set fire to the rear turret and the port inner engine and damaged the intercommunication system. The rear gunner was injured by splinters in the face and slightly burnt and the mid-upper was hit by a machine-gun bullet in the leg. The attack came from astern well down and as soon as the pilot saw the tracer he commenced a corkscrew port, losing height rapidly to gain extra

---

* Frankfurt – Fifty-three Lancasters lost on those three ops. Berlin – 243 on those seven.

speed, having a full load on. Both gunners saw a Ju88 come in from astern down, but rear gunner could not fire as guns had been damaged and MU could not get guns to bear. E/A broke away down and again attacked from same position opening fire at 600 yards and closing in to 100 yards. E/A's trace all passed above the bomber and he broke away astern down and was not seen again. The pilot resumed course on three engines and bombed the target from a very low altitude before returning to base.

Visibility clear but dark. No moon, flares or searchlights. No indication on any special apparatus. Damage to own aircraft: rear turret badly smashed. Port inner engine u/s. MU turret and fuselage holed in many places. Intercom shot away. No rounds fired by either gunner. Bombs were dropped on written instructions from navigator when over centre of target area.

Pilot Officer Len Glover was awarded the DFC for carrying on to bomb from a very low altitude while reading a note from his navigator, after being swept from stem to stern by cannon and machine guns and corkscrewing out of trouble on three engines in a fully loaded aircraft – defenceless against what was obviously a skilled and experienced foe – before returning to base. He was back on duty nine days later, on 2 January, flying to Berlin with two new gunners.

Glover's tail-end Charlie, the splintered and slightly burnt Sergeant G. Brown, was re-crewed with another lucky skipper, Flying Officer Bill Reid, and was also soon out bombing again at Stettin, on 5 January.

Chapter One

Her Name Was Robert

By the time No. 9 Squadron took delivery of its first Lancasters, in August 1942, there were eight other squadrons already flying this magnificent new machine and its fame had been spread by the first Lancaster units, Nos. 44 and 97 Squadrons. They had gone a very long way to Augsburg in daylight with twelve Lancs, led by Squadron Leader John Nettleton, VC, and come back with seven.

Factories struggling with a new set of production problems were managing something around fifty Lancasters a month during that summer, building up to over a hundred by the end of the year. As losses averaged almost twenty a month in 1942, we can see that re-equipping bomber squadrons with the latest aircraft was no more than a steady business. Even so, numbers were building and the objective of Bomber Command's C-in-C, Air Chief Marshal Harris, of massed bombers attacking together, was coming closer as a regular thing.

At the beginning of the war – and for most of its first two years – skippers of bombers were told what the targets were for the night, the weather forecast and the opposition they were likely to meet. They were given a general take-off time and a point at which to cross the English coast, but after that it was up to them, as long as they could expect to be returning before dawn.

Skipper and navigator would work out where to enter enemy territory across the Dutch coast and the rest of the route, and how they would attack. Experience, personality and attitude on the day would influence their decisions.

On a dark or cloudy night, with no possibility of matching the terrain below to the map on his table, or the stars in his sextant if he had one, the navigator had to work on dead reckoning. It didn't need much of a side wind to knock an aircraft ten, twenty, or fifty miles off course. It was unrealistic, if not out of the question, to expect bombers in bad weather to hit a specified area of a city, or a specified city at all, yet the crews were given very specific targets – certain factories, steel works, power stations, company head offices. Any effect the bombers might have had was further diminished by the long list of targets for any one night, so that only nine or ten aircraft went to each, when and if they got there, making them easier to pick off and less likely to create lasting damage.

Matching this was the attitude of the German defenders, as put in *The Luftwaffe War Diaries*:

'The Luftwaffe calculated that even with a small force of fighters it could repel any air attacks on the homeland by day, and that by night the bombers would fail to hit their targets. But the overwhelming strength of the Allies, with new navigational and target-finding methods, led to concentrated bombing even by night.

'Though the German night–fighter arm achieved mounting success, this failed to keep pace with the increasing strength of the bomber formations. The *Himmelbett*[*] procedure, by which a single night-fighter was put into contact with a bomber by means of close ground control, functioned satisfactorily so long as the bombers arrived and departed over a broad front and strung out in time. The later tactics of compact bomber streams could

---

[*] *Himmelbett* – literally sky-bed, was a name coined by one of its pioneers, and it stuck.

only be met by means of independent fighters carrying their own radar.'

In April to July 1942, flying from their grass airfield at Honington, Suffolk, according to the routines outlined above, No. 9 Squadron had lost the equivalent, in Wellington aircraft and crews, of nearly two entire squadrons' operational strength. The thought of the new bomber was a welcome inspiration. Away went the Wellingtons; in came the Lancasters.

On 7 August the squadron set up at Waddington, Lincolnshire, where there were facilities such as tarmac runways; on the ninth the pilots started training. A young fellow called Harry Irons had just arrived straight from gunnery school, without going through an OTU (Operational Training Unit):

'They (the converting crews) were teaching themselves, really. There didn't seem to be any organised instruction. There were some very experienced men there, but they'd never been in a Lancaster before.'

There were big differences for the crew as well, from Wellington days. Bomb aiming had been becoming a specialised trade, rather than the second pilot or the observer doing it, and it was completely so now, with the new and excellent, semi-automatic Mark XIV bombsight. Some Wellington front gunners, like Dennis Mason, retrained as bomb aimers:

'I flew in Oxfords dropping practice bombs and map-reading and then I had my first flight in one of these new Lancasters. It was a disaster. The pilot overshot on his first landing approach, with me watching in the front turret. He called me back and we made another five attempts to land, including one where we caught the undercart on the boundary fence. At last we crash-landed on the grass and I jumped out from the astrodome, carrying my parachute. I should have had it open, with the difference in height between jumping from a Wellington and a Lanc.'

There was also a dedicated flight engineer rather than a second pilot, to look after the complexities of the Lancaster's four Rolls-Royce Merlins. At the start of the war, gunnery had been something the wireless operator did in his spare time, or the captain would pick up some innocent ground crew lad and tell him he had a new job today. Now, gunners had a six-month training course, and wireless operating was definitely a full-time occupation. Navigators were still navigators, but no longer called observers.

Lancaster R5916 WS/R-Robert, brand new of course, went on her first op on 13 September 1942 to Bremen, skippered by Canadian Flying Officer Ken Mackenzie with an all-ex-Wellington crew except for the flight engineer. Through the rest of that autumn, No. 9 Squadron went to an assortment of targets. Some were hard, German business. One, to France, was special for several reasons.

There was some very unusual daylight training over five days in early October, in low formation flying with several other squadrons. No. 9 Squadron was to form the first wing on an unspecified attack with Nos. 49 and 61 Squadrons, and few, if any, of the pilots had had experience of close formations. Against widely held private expectations and a certain amount of talk from mid-upper gunners about sitting in a boiled egg while your top was sliced off, there were no accidents to the Lancasters. Harry Irons:

'There were ninety of us, flying in a gaggle at about twenty feet, around Lincoln, over The Wash, and these Spitfires came at us.

They came in from behind in a mock attack and we were too low to take evasive action. As the Spits tried to break away they hit the slipstream of ninety Lancs. If we'd been at a hundred feet they'd have been all right. As it was, some of them just flipped over and went straight into the deck.'

Ken Mackenzie in R-Robert and eight others trained until they had proved they could fly at zero feet, almost touching each other, at full speed for hours on end. Then they were told the target: the Schneider works at Le Creusot, the biggest iron and steel manufactory in France, the Krupps of the south, making guns, engines and armour.

There were ninety-four Lancasters going, six were to hit the power station, while the rest went for the various mills and factory buildings. Operations Record Book (ORB) for No. 9 Squadron:

'Flying at 0 feet over the Channel, ran into sea fog which cleared 40 minutes later with all aircraft still in sight and squadron formation regained by French coast.'

For Irons, flying with the legendary Dick Stubbs, that was almost the end of it. Another Lancaster swerved across them, which forced their aircraft into an instant half roll. She went through 90 degrees in less than the wink of an eye and everyone swore that the downward wingtip was in the water. Stubbs got her back, brilliant flyer that he was, and resumed formation as if nothing had happened.

Almost immediately, there was a terrific bang, the front Perspex had a great hole in it and Tom Parrington, flight engineer, was covered in blood. Harry Irons:

'A very large French seagull had come through the Perspex and Tom was knocked out for quite a while. Nothing else happened after that. We were in a loose gaggle about a mile wide, easy meat for any fighters, but we never saw any and it was crystal clear weather. We could see for miles and miles. We never saw our escorts either; we were supposed to have a couple of hundred Spitfires but they didn't turn up.'

French people waved cheerily as the bombers flashed overhead. They bombed at between 5,000 and 2,500 feet and, for the most part, accurately. ORB:

'Buildings were disintegrating in all parts of the factory and, with the exception of a few near-misses, almost all bombs fell across the works, creating tremendous damage.'

This was true, and a very successful raid it was, but not entirely without the damage that in modern times is called collateral. Harry Irons:

'Quite a few of the bombs fell short, onto the housing estate which was at one end of the factory. There were plenty of civilian properties destroyed as well as the target.'

Ken Mackenzie reported, 'Town completely obscured by smoke'. Post-raid photographs would confirm the airmen's opinion.

Some ops, like the series of raids on Italian ports and production centres to reinforce the army's fight at El Alamein, came up against light defences and had to be classed as relatively easy, if long. Crews reported an uneventful trip to Genoa on 6 November, with quite a large amount of light flak which was ineffective. Slight amounts of heavy flak were fired seemingly at random.

What the Italian gunners could not achieve, the thoughtlessness of RAF's head office planners could achieve for them. The crews of No. 9 Squadron were back from their nine-hour flights on the 6 November at around 0700 hours, briefed for another op at 1500 hours, and away again to Genoa at 1730 hours. Mackenzie was in WS/R on her twelfth op, as he had been hours before, having skippered eight of those twelve trips. Coming home from their second Italian long haul without a proper break in between, Flying Officer Mackenzie, DFC, piloting R5916 WS/R-Robert, collided in mid-air with the Lancaster flown by the newly promoted Pilot Officer Macdonald. These were both Wellington veterans and very experienced pilots, crashing on the southern edge of the aerodrome. There were no survivors. Mackenzie's crew was the same as their first in R-Robert, with the exception of the flight engineer.

The squadron was given a stand-down for a day, before ops to Hamburg on the 9 November.

The next WS/R, ED308, flew first to Turin, then Mannheim, Duisburg, and Duisburg again, all with Sergeant Doolan and crew. Captain's notes, 8 January 1943:

'Aircraft received direct hit from heavy flak near Duisburg, 1930 hrs, 20,000ft, on R/Gunner's turret, causing death of rear gunner (Sgt R.W. Robinson). Special praise due to F/Engineer, W/Op and Navigator for getting R/Gunner out of turret and administering first aid at great risk to themselves.'

Gunner Harry Irons was available as a replacement for Sergeant Robinson, his ex-Wellington pilot Flight Lieutenant Dick Stubbs, DFC and some of the crew having completed their tours. Irons:

'The skipper came to me and we shook hands. He said, "Harry, I'm off, but I wish you luck and hope you survive the rest of your tour". Which was nice of him. (In fact, Harry J. Irons, DFC, would survive two tours, but Stubbs would be killed in a flying accident.)

'Reggie Robinson, called Robbie, was a bit older than me; he'd be 20 or 21, from Brixton. They brought him back but there was nothing left of him apart from some of his upper body. We gunners knew each other. We went to his funeral. The parents had declined the offer to see his body. They wanted to remember him as he was. His skipper was Sgt Doolan, who was famous as a pilot who couldn't land. Aircrew considered landing an important skill and weren't keen on flying with him. So he came in the mess and said they'd put a nice new turret on his Lanc and would I like to get in it. Some of my pals said, "you're not going with him, are you?" I said there wasn't anybody else.'

They did indeed put a nice new turret on ED308 WS/R, but transferred the entire aircraft to No. 50 Squadron, where she became VN/J-Jig and flew all the way through that year and well into the next, at last going down on the night of 18/19 March 1944 at Frankfurt. Harry Irons joined Doolan and carried on.

The third Robert, ED501 WS/R, arrived on squadron in February 1943. ORB, 9 February:

'Slight intermittent rain during dawn and early morning, otherwise fine. Again Wilhelmshaven was to have been the target for nine crews. They were briefed and due to take off at 2330 hours. The cancellation was made at 2250 hours when the crews were already at the aircraft. A night cross-country by a new crew force-landed in Anglesey.'

On the 10th:

'For the third time in succession Wilhelmshaven was chosen as the target. The cancellation was given at approx. 1730 hours when the crews were waiting to go out to their aircraft.'

At last, on 11 February, Wilhelmshaven was attacked, that fateful place where No. 9 Squadron had lost five Wellingtons out of nine on a grey December day in 1939. There had to be a certain frisson about Wilhelmshaven but they didn't lose anybody this time.

'Weather conditions were such that the WAMGAMUI Technique had to be employed.' ORB scribe's spelling was poor on this point, but Wanganui was an experimental (at this time) type of 'sky-marking' flare for use in ten-tenths cloud. The Pathfinders also had the new H2S air-to-ground radar and dropped their parachute flares on indications from that temperamental source. 'Crews reported large flashes below the cloud after bombing and a glow as they left the target area.'

For the first time, H2S worked well as a blind-bombing aid and so the marking was spot on. The flashes and the glow came from a German navy ammunition dump which went up with a terrific explosion and caused devastation all around.

U-boat pens on the French coast at Lorient and St Nazaire were now high on the list for attack. In fact, they were sometimes given priority over German industrial targets, much to the C-in-C's disgust because he didn't yet have a bomb which could penetrate the concrete, 18 feet thick and more, and he was anxious to start using his new navigation aids, Oboe and H2S, on the Ruhr. The Oboe system, like the older Gee, was based on transmissions from ground stations and so was of limited range, but it was highly accurate. It had drawbacks that meant that only a few aircraft could use it at a time and then not in all circumstances, but it was a great improvement.

Despite Harris's protestations, the prime objective for the moment, according to the Air Ministry Directive Letter, was the effective devastation of the whole area in which the submarines, their maintenance facilities, and the services, power, water, light, communications and other resources on which their operations depend were located.

The U-boat menace had lately increased. At any one time there could be twenty-eight U-boats docked at Lorient alone, safe beneath their concrete roofs, impenetrable to all known forms of aerial attack. The most successful U-boats of the war, from top scorer U-48 to seventh best U-37, which between them sank 313 ships, all operated from Lorient where anti-aircraft defences included almost three hundred guns.

Doolan, in the new WS/R, saw; 'In clear moonlight, river and built-up area visually identified. Several very large red fires concentrated in town and dock area with pall of thick smoke up to 6,000 ft.' This was a big raid, almost 500 bombers dropping 1,000 tons of bombs; while Lorient itself suffered badly, the U-boat pens did not.

WS/R helped Milan suffer badly too next night – Doolan again – then another Lorient with Sergeant Ralph Brown. His crew was unique in the squadron and possibly in the whole of Bomber Command. Although mostly in their early twenties, five of the seven were married and, on a night in April, with the squadron's Bombing Leader Ron Higginson, DFM, filling in for the regular man, that made six. Their end was witnessed by Ken Dagnall, bomb aimer with McCubbin and a future flyer in another WS/R that lasted rather longer. The scene was the Gulf of Gascony, 22 April, mine-laying near St-Jean-de-Luz, Bayonne:

'There was only half a dozen Lancs there and the moon was shining brightly. We circled twice around a lighthouse on the Spanish border, then we started in on our run, which was one minute forty-eight seconds. We could see the anti-aircraft fire ahead. They were throwing everything at us, light flak, heavy flak, machine guns, everything. The aircraft in front of us was blown out of the sky and we flew right through the explosion. We were shitting bricks, absolutely shitting bricks, and they never hit us with a single round. Not a bullet.'

Back to February with WS/R when there followed an inconclusive Wilhelmshaven and a cloudy Bremen with Sergeant Doolan, then into March with Warrant Officer White to Nürnberg, where there were some big hits on the factories of MAN and Siemens. New Zealander Arthur White lasted only a month before he and all his crew died under the guns of a night-fighter over Utrecht.

WS/R was back with Doolan on 9 March for Munich, where the BMW factories were hit, and next night for mine-laying in the Baltic, and Stuttgart made three in a row, skippered by the Rhodesian, Flight Sergeant John Walsh. He was lucky and lasted a long time, but not quite lucky enough. After three months at it, come 4 April, he and his crew must have thought they could fly through another few weeks and it would be over. A fighter intercepted them near Neumünster, about 20 miles from the target at Kiel and it was indeed over.

Once more with the very lucky Sergeant Doolan, WS/R flew on a fourth consecutive night, this time to Essen, where the huge Krupp works took a lot of damage, and on 29 March to Berlin, where there were considerable bomber losses for little return. There was another Essen trip, and one to Duisburg, then the luck ran out when Doolan handed ED501 WS/R-Robert over to his squadron commander.

The new boss had arrived at No. 9 Squadron, 5 Group RAF Bomber Command, on 15 March 1943. Wing Commander Kenneth Brooke Farley Smith, DSO, was a 30-year-old regular from before the war, an Oxford graduate and a man who took his responsibilities very seriously indeed, beginning with three Lancaster trips as passenger, one of them to Berlin. A squadron CO, invariably a pilot, was not obliged to go on ops at all, as passenger or skipper, but, of course, most of them did. Ken Dagnall remembered it well:

'The squadron lost five aircraft in action in the first nine days of that April. We suddenly became one of the senior crews and we'd only been on four operations. The Wingco (Smith) had us all assembled in a room for briefing. Normally, a squadron should be a hundred-plus men, needing the village hall to meet in. We fitted in somewhere like your dining room at home. He said, "I'm going with you tonight, to find out what's wrong". Which was a bit daft. He wasn't going to find out what was wrong that way. What was wrong was that Jerry was shooting us down, that's what was wrong.'

Wing Commander Smith, DSO, mentioned twice in despatches, did find out what was wrong. He never came back. He went in near Mainz with an experienced crew and, to make matters even worse, a second Dicky (new pilot on work-experience trip), on 10 April, in ED501 WS/R, seventeen ops in two months, one of only seven Lancs the squadron had been able to send to Frankfurt. Ken Dagnall:

'The Wingco might have been like quite a few of them, I think, senior officers brought up on biplanes and Empire business, you know, fighting the old fuzzy-wuzzies in the Middle East somewhere. They were fearless and determined, but perhaps not all of them had grasped the essentials of flying at 20,000 feet at night over Germany.'

WS/R the fourth, ED838, was driven on her first op by a skipper also on his first, the diminutive Trinidadian Pilot Officer George Nunez. It was a mining trip – 'vegetables planted in allotted position, 2,000 feet'

– on 28 April 1943. Such ops were usually referred to as gardening, and the mines as vegetables, and they were relatively less attritional than the real business, such as raids on Happy Valley, the Ruhr, which is where Nunez and WS/R went two nights later, to Essen. A force of 190 Lancasters and 105 Halifaxes did well in the cloud, hitting the Krupp factories and many other buildings, but among the twelve bombers that went down was ED838 WS/R, lost without trace, all her men commemorated at Runnymede.

There would be no more men killed in Lancasters designated WS/R until New Year's Day 1945. Here is a list of the unlucky ones before No. 9 Squadron took delivery of the main vehicle in our story, EE136.

7 November 1942
R5916 WS/R; crashed at home after Genoa.
Flying Officer Kenneth Alexander Mackenzie, DFC
Sergeant James John Taaffe
Sergeant Arthur Reuben Billington
Sergeant Kenneth Thomas John Adams
Sergeant Roy Ernest Werren
Sergeant David John Wicks
Sergeant Herbert Richard Willacy

8 January 1943
ED308 WS/R; Duisburg
Sergeant Reginald Warren Robinson, rear gunner

10 April 1943
ED501 WS/R; Frankfurt
Wing Commander Kenneth Brooke Farley Smith, DSO
Sergeant William Thomson
Flying Officer Arnold James Turner

Flying Officer Bernard James Smith
Sergeant Gordon Arthur Taylor
Sergeant Louis Stanley Fiddes
Pilot Officer Roy Victor Charles Pleasance
Sergeant Allan Gaskell Stone, second pilot

30 April 1943
ED838 WS/R; Essen
Pilot Officer George Albert Nunez
Sergeant Cecil Howard Collins
Sergeant Alvery Beard
Sergeant Edward Francis Doolittle
Sergeant Reginald Arthur Knapman
Sergeant Jack Bayliss
Sergeant Dennis Robert Barber

Chapter Two

Who Were Those Men?

There are many statistics of the bombing war, with different ways of looking at them and variations in how they were compiled. In round numbers, Lancasters accounted for about a third of all operations flown in the war and something over a third of all losses, although they didn't come into service in any numbers until the summer of 1942.

Looking at the end of the war, we can assume that most of the Lancasters delivered to squadrons in April and May 1945 didn't do much operational flying, and so we can say (in round numbers again) that 6,000 Lancasters were made available for duty in the war, of which 3,400 were lost flying 150,000 missions. This gives a Lancaster life expectancy, averaged across the war, of twenty-five operations. The actual figure, in life rather than accounts books, was much nearer twenty.

Again across the war, approximately 125,000 aircrew served in Bomber Command, volunteer joiners or men already on squadron when the war began, of whom 55,500 became fatal casualties, while 10,000 became POWs. Another 2,000+ were wounded in action but got home, and a similar number suffered bodily harm in home-based accidents. We don't have figures for aircrew arriving and surviving in the heavy years of 1943/44, but we can be sure that the percentages and proportions were even worse. It is said that the only job more dangerous was in a U-boat crew.

From the time when the really big raids began, mid-1942, through to the end of 1944, HQ regarded losses of less than five bombers in a hundred, on any given op, as being a kind of par for the course. Any more than 5 per cent and special reasons had to be looked for and explained.

At squadron level, aircrew had no figures to go on but they could see what was happening around them. Anyone completing a tour of ops – 200 operational flying hours at first, translated later into thirty completed ops – would know that a whole squadron's worth of aircraft and crew had been lost in the five months or so it took him to do that. Front-line squadrons in 1943 were losing a Lancaster a week, and it was only slightly better in 1944. So, sitting in the mess looking at this week's newly empty chairs, you had to tell yourself that it was going to be the other fellow who got the chop, not you.

Sitting at a desk at HQ, Air Chief Marshal Harris and his staff had to balance what could be done with what was needed; using what was available and sustainable in terms of crews and machines. With greatly improved rates of aircraft production and aircrew training, that statistic of 5 per cent could be regarded as acceptable, in a very brutal line of work.

That was to say, it was acceptable to those who did not fly in bombers, or who did not love those who flew in bombers, who did not repair and maintain bombers, or who did not work on aerodromes.

There were arguments about it in the mess. Some crews were lost on their first trip; therefore, some would have the luck to survive the thirty. That was reassuring to those who felt themselves to be very lucky. Another way of looking at it was to say that the lost Lancasters were replaced so, each time you went, you were one of many again, just as mathematically unlikely to be the one who had a prang, bought a packet, bought the farm, went for a Burton, got the chop. Was killed.

Yet another way was to say that it was like batting in cricket. If you scored nineteen not out, you were more likely to reach thirty than you had been when you came in on nought. The point was that there was no real pattern to it. New boys, sprog crews, were more likely to be lost than old hands, that was observably true, but the powers that be counteracted that by giving the worst jobs to the old hands. Also, some of the old hands got over confident. And, there was that little matter of luck.

In the early days of the air war, allocation of crewmen to captain was not a fully organised business, but rather a mixture of captain's choice, Hobson's choice and the art of the possible. It was always desirable to have a settled crew with a trusted captain as a smoothly functioning unit and, as everything grew, technology improved and the job got bigger and even more dangerous, that desire for the bomber crew as a cohesive team became ever more important.

RAF Bomber Command never imposed a full Lancaster crew on a captain – at least, such a thing was not heard of. Occasionally, as in the case of the squadron commanding officer deciding he would go on one of his irregular trips, a captain might impose an extempore crew on himself, but otherwise the rule was that the crew should be – as far as possible – self-selecting.

Crews were not allotted nor selected by any scientific method, because there was no method to use. The Americans were experimenting with psychological testing to see if that might help explain why pilots with no obvious differences between them could have such fatal differences in their operational careers, but the complexities and inter-dependencies of a bomber crew were far beyond the state of psychometric practice at that time, or any time.

By mid-1943, the crewing-up routine was well established. Inside a large room, part-trained aircrew stood and sat about in their groups. The bomb aimers were together, navigators together, wireless operators together, and the pilots started drifting between them. It was like a quiet party with no drinks, one of those parties where the idea is to circulate, not to have a good time.

At the party, this skipper decided he wanted this wireless operator, but the w/op didn't quite feel right about the skipper. No go. Just don't fancy it. Sorry. But another wireless operator thought differently and agreed. Good. Gradually the groups diffused and mingled. Gradually a few settlements were made. Crews began to assemble themselves.

Each man was making decisions – using no information and no experience – that could well seal his fate. Luck had something to do with whether you came back from an op or not, but the pilot, or the navigator, or the gunners, or the engineer, or any one member of the team, could have even more to do with it.

Even with the system in place, some crew assembly still happened at random. One pilot who had fiddled his age on joining the RAF and so was barely nineteen at the crewing up stage, was understandably worried about how others might see him.

'I found one of my crew at a railway station on a bleak November night. There was quite a crowd of airmen standing around in overcoats. I said aloud, but to myself, "Nobody will fly with me," and a boy turned to me and said, "I will". The boy became our rear gunner.'

The first gathering usually put together pilot, navigator, bomb aimer and wireless op, closely followed by the two gunners. While the pilot's training took the longest, starting on a Tiger Moth, often abroad, and flying a Lancaster to Berlin almost three years later, gunners had only six months to learn their life-and-death trade. This is a little curious because, on his first operational flight, a gunner could become *pro tem* captain of his aircraft, issuing orders to the pilot to dive, climb, turn, whatever, after spotting an incoming night-fighter.

In among all the authority, ranks, discipline and traditional officers-and-men attitudes, there was this strange kind of democracy. Just as the lowliest corporal on ground crew could stop a bomber taking off if he wasn't satisfied with some technical aspect, so the fate of a bomber aircraft and seven men could rest on the reactions and judgement of an eighteen-year-old who had had no training whatever in such matters. Of course, he was trained to fire his gun, and some of the techniques employed in that connection were imaginative to say the least.

In an aircraft hangar were arranged ten gun turrets in rows of five, facing the long walls. They had intercom between themselves and between them and the instructor, who was in a little cubicle by the door. On each long wall was painted a continuous white, snaking, looping line, perhaps modelled on the wanderings of a drunken snail, more likely attempting to reproduce the effects on gun-aiming made by a corkscrewing bomber trying to get away from a fighter that was trying to avoid being shot at.

Trainee gunners concentrated here on turret manipulation along the twisty lines, like the game where a metal ring must be taken up and down and round a wiggly electrified wire without touching it and ringing the bell, only the gunners had to be quick. Turret movement was the one advantage a bomber had over a fighter whose pilot had to line up his aircraft for a shot, while the turret gunner could mostly get a shot in whatever the relative positions of the combatants.

Mastery of turret driving was the trainee gunner's goal and evidence of achievement was unofficially shown with a pencil attached to the end of the gun. Using only his turret controls, the trainee would make a drawing of a familiar reproductive organ or, in the case of the inhibited, sign his name. Breakdowns were expected, so trainees had to learn to assemble two different types of machine gun, parts mixed together, blindfolded.

With these examinations passed, the students went up in the air. Four trainee gunners would be in an Oxford, or an Avro Anson, taking it in turns to operate the gun turret, firing cine film at pursuing RAF fighters pretending to be Germans, or live rounds at a drogue being towed abeam of them by a Fairey Battle or some such. After fifteen or so hours of this, spread over a month, it was off to practice in a Wellington.

So, here was a crew of six. They'd had a few weeks' basic training at an Initial Training Wing, where they'd swapped their RAF boots for aircrew shoes as soon as they'd learned to march. They then forgot most of the rest of it. They'd had a good quantity of theoretical training and rigorous tests in their respective trades to make sure they knew the job backwards, the idea being that vital matters would become instincts. Even so, all the training in the world could never be enough. There had to be a judgement. Somebody had to decide when you were ready to leave school and get out into the big wide world where Germans tried to kill you.

Towards the end of the Wellington time they were introduced to a new game with the snappy title of Fighter Affiliation. Affiliate, literally to adopt as the son of, generally to connect oneself with, was the complete opposite of what they actually did. In daylight, a Spitfire or a Hurricane with a cine camera and a pilot intent on a bit of sport would attack the bomber and the bomber pilot would desperately try to disconnect himself from the fighter while the gunners called the corkscrews and dives and tried to hit the fighter with their own cine film.

The results indicated more than the skills of the players. A gunner who was not such a good shot or turret-driver, or a bomber pilot who lacked confidence in violent dives and turns, would give the fighter pilot an advantage, but timing and teamwork were just as important. The rear gunner in particular was the chief of defence for the aircraft; teamwork with the pilot had to be instinctive and trust had to be total. Here is one gunner's memory of it:

'In fighter affiliation you'd be just flying along and then a fighter would sneak up on you from below, or all of a sudden dive out of the clouds and come at you. We were told they were trainee pilots, but I don't know if they were. Our job as gunners was to get him on the camera, and to tell the skipper which way to go. Whoever saw the fighter first, rear or mid-upper, shouted the order. You dived into the attacker, towards where he was coming from. Then the skipper would chuck the aircraft about, so we got chucked about as well, and there was quite a lot of G. It was difficult, really.'

At night, fighter affiliation was fish of a different kettle. Clayton Moore was a Canadian gunner we shall meet later in the story:

'We had been navigating a complicated route for about two hours and I had successfully lost a fighter by calling on Bill (Siddle, pilot) to throw the aircraft around. I was congratulating myself on my vigilance when, to my amazement, I was suddenly confronted by a Beaufighter sitting 50 yards astern with all its navigation lights on. The cockpit then lit up like the Palais on a Saturday night, its two occupants grinning at me and giving me the thumbs down.'

Exercises were no real preparation for the hours and hours of continuous searching which gunners had to do on a long trip over Germany, when it was so easy to lapse into that waking coma when eyes were open but messages were not reaching the brain. Many crews, fully aware of this problem, developed their own methods of regular alarm calls.

Fighter 'affiliation', whether with friendly Spits or unfriendly Germans, would become a regular part of ordinary operational life but, before that, a crew would be off to a Conversion Unit, where pilots were adapted from the two-engined Wellington to four engines, often in a Stirling, a cumbersome beast largely relegated to training after being tried and found wanting over Germany. Crews would move on to Lancasters and Halifaxes, and they would most of them recall the Stirling with distaste.

The flight engineer came on board at this point. He was a pilot in reserve as well as airborne mechanic and systems controller. Flight engineers were expected to have a full understanding of the aircraft's abilities, requirements and responses, and to be able to fly it straight and level, having had a few hours' practice on the ground on a Link trainer. Pilots were human. They could get migraines, or feel sick, or be killed come to that, and the engineer might have to do the job. It was the same procedure as before; engineers in the hall, pilot went in and walked around, having a chat here and there. A pilot in his early days of flying a very large, four-engined aircraft needed things to go right in the cockpit, especially at take-off and landing, which were the most dangerous aspects of flying anyway, but particularly so in a Stirling.

For most of the crew, conversion to the larger aircraft was not a problem. The equipment was much the same as they were used to. For the pilots at this stage of training there were obvious challenges – four engines instead of two and a much bigger piece of business altogether. Also there was a lot of night flying and a great many aircraft doing circuits at any one time. These hazards could sometimes seem worse than flying over Germany, and there were many accidents. In 1943 alone, there were 503 aircraft – almost all Wellingtons – lost by Operational Training Units, often with fatalities of crew; and another 252 Lancasters, Halifaxes and Stirlings, lost by Conversion Units. In 1944, the equivalent figures were 352 and 467.

Everybody knew that flying in bombers was dangerous. Just how dangerous was not always perfectly apparent to those heading towards operational life, until they got there. An independent observer like the station medical officer might have noticed a pattern in the morale of these crews, these men who, whenever they flew, had to obliterate their most basic instinct, that of self-preservation, so they could do their work.

Generally speaking, spirits would be at their highest when they knew nothing about it, when they were going on their first few ops. These flights would be so full of novelty, such an amazing and mind-boggling experience, that most aircrew would feel no fear as such. Real fear, if it is to have a disabling effect, needs time and space to work. Like a child on the ghost train at the seaside, aircrew at first might feel a frantic kind of excitement-cum-fright but they didn't usually have the room in their souls to be genuinely rendered useless by fear. They were too busy, anyway. Flying an op in a Lancaster was a highly complex business for every crew member and, until they got used to it, there was never a thinking moment other than about the job in hand. Here's mid-upper gunner Harry Irons on his first:

'So off we went to Düsseldorf and I'd never been so frightened in my life. I didn't know what was going on. Never been to OTU and Stubbs (captain) said, "You'll learn as you go along", so that was the extent of my operational education. I couldn't credit the flak and the searchlights and all the aircraft blowing up. I had the best view from my turret. We were hit by flak and on top of that we had a lot of engine trouble with the Lanc. I was in a daze when we got back. But Stubbs was right. You did get used to it.'

If they lasted five or six ops, spirits often began to sink as the enormity of their task became increasingly obvious. The novelty had worn off; they had become battle-scarred professionals in a short few weeks and, like all veterans, had come to recognise the price their profession had to pay. Perhaps the worst time for morale was around halfway through the tour, when a crew might be fully justified in thinking that their luck was due to run out. Once that dark period was passed, a devil-may-care kind of attitude could take over. The bastards haven't got me yet and they're not going to, not now, not when I've got this far.

Then, before the last few ops of the tour, a certain dread might creep in. Are the fates going to let me through, or are they going to let me think I'm through before having the last laugh? For some, running inside all of this was a thread of addiction, to the risk, and to the nerve jangling exhilaration of doing something about smiting the enemy.

Meanwhile, the enemy was doing his own smiting. Flak (anti-aircraft artillery, abbreviated from *Fliegerabwehrkanonen,* flyer defence gun) was always a danger, ever present, at every target, on the way there and on the way back. You could see the light flak coming, coloured tracer shooting upwards towards you and, hopefully, past. The heavy sort, individual shells primed to explode at a certain height, you would know nothing about at night until it happened, a single shell blowing your wing off or the puff of smoke that missed.

A crew who strayed off track might happen over a well defended urban area on their own, a deadly fate, and losses were often suffered this way. The straight and level bombing run was a gift to the flak gunners and, especially in the minds of the bomber crews, the gift was wrapped and beribboned by the extra time they had to fly after 'bombs gone', waiting for their photoflash bomb to explode and their camera to click. This was not only to help RAF Intelligence assess the damage. It also proved that a crew had been where they said they had been and that they were indeed straight and level as per procedure.

Fighters were a different kind of silent menace, looking for the surprise attack and, if they achieved that surprise and could shoot straight, very likely indeed to score. The exhausts from a Lancaster's engines, full of sparks, could be noticed from a mile and a half away. On a clear night, a fighter pilot could close in and see the bomber silhouetted against the stars to confirm the signal his wireless operator was getting on the radar, the Lichtenstein set. Once the fighter fastened on, provided he was cautious about being spotted, and after maybe stalking his victim for quite some time, the odds were hugely in his favour. The Lancaster, comparatively slow and clumsy, duty bound to head in a straight line for the target, was armed only with rifle bullets, .303 inch calibre (about 8mm). The fighter had those too, but also cannon shells, 20mm or sometimes 30mm in diameter.

The only hope the bombers had was in the eyes of the crew, almost always the gunners' eyes except, in 1943/44, for Monica. Monica was a form of radar meant to pick up enemy fighters and, quite often, she worked. She could not discriminate between RAF and Luftwaffe – all aircraft were the same to her – nor could she tell where they were coming from. She could only give their distance. The closer together her pip-pip sounds, the nearer was the aircraft.

It was just as well that wireless operators and the other crew members didn't know that Monica had developed into a very attractive lady, *une femme fatale*, in fact. The Germans had devised an instrument called Flensburg that picked up Monica's radar signals and used them to home in on the transmitting aircraft from as much as 45 miles away. After a Ju88 equipped with Flensburg landed by mistake at Woodbridge, the radar scientists quickly worked out what it was for and Monica was retired from active service in September 1944.

There was another device called Boozer that picked up transmissions from the German fighter radar, Lichtenstein, without offering anything in return. This would have been an unappreciated advantage over Monica except for Boozer's frequent false alarms. It was one of those better-than-nothing magic boxes, regarded with a mixture of suspicion and hope by aircrew. When it worked, if the Boozer-equipped aircraft was being held in a night-fighter's Lichtenstein, a yellow lamp lit up, and the pilot threw his machine about until the lamp went out.

In the bomber stream, neither 'special apparatus' could tell friend from foe and so warning lights and pip-pip sounds tended only to increase tension, which was already high enough, rather than gave any kind of definite warning that could be acted upon with confidence. It was not unknown for experienced crews to 'turn the bloody thing off' and rely on the old technology of gunner's eyeball.

SECRET: No. 9 Squadron Combat Report
Unidentified T/E (twin-engined) A/C sighted starboard bow 1000 yards silhouetted by fires, which turned in on curve of pursuit. Mid upper gunner gave order to commence diving turn to starboard and at same time opened fire at 500 yards. E/A closed to 400 yards then broke away without having opened fire.
Captain F/O Hadland. MU gunner Sgt Tirel 300 rounds.

Darkness was the bomber's friend as well as the fighter's. Darkness allowed the fighter to get close, but darkness might fool him into getting into range, where the four machine guns at the back and the two in the mid-upper turret could pour quite a volume of rifle bullets.

SECRET: No. 9 Squadron Combat Report
...enemy attacked at 800 yards from green fine quarter and was seen by rear gunner as a result of its tracer... enemy sighted again 100 yards range... enemy aircraft held off at 400 yards while our aircraft completed three orbits... then attacked from green quarter down in shallow climb. Our rear gunner opened fire at 200 yards, ceasing at 150 yards firing 200 rounds. Hits were observed on fuselage. Enemy aircraft broke off and was not seen again. One minute later a large flash was observed on the ground approximately four miles astern.
Captain F/Sgt Thomas. Rear Gunner F/Sgt Morgan.

SECRET: No. 9 Squadron Combat Report
...at 20,000 feet over the sea MU gunner sighted a Ju88... starboard beam below, 500 yards... climbed to same level... seen to orbit at

500 yards and made an attack from port bow opening fire at approx 350 yards... mid-upper turret u/s owing to oil leak... our aircraft continued steep diving turn to port... it appeared that Ju88 had difficulty in laying his aim... our rear gunner fired three bursts at a comparatively steady target. The Ju88 was seen to dive steeply away... short while later the gunners and bomb aimer saw a red glow followed by a short bright explosion at sea level.

Captain F/O Wilmot. MU gunner Sgt Pearce. Rear gunner Sgt Taylor; fired 800 rounds, no stoppages.

SECRET: No. 9 Squadron Combat Report

T/E E/A (enemy aircraft) shining a turbine lamp* from nose position approached Lancaster from starboard quarter and below from direction of a crashed bomber. Fighter came in to 1000 yards developing stern attack, closing to 500-600 yards. Rear gunner ordered corkscrew to port and simultaneously fired approx 150 rounds. Tracer was seen to enter enemy aircraft which, without firing a shot, stalled and spun down and was seen to explode on the ground. Fire could still be seen burning ten minutes later.

Captain F/O Anstee. Rear gunner Sgt Collins.

The Germans seemingly also had inexperienced pilots who would never become experienced. Even so, while one Lancaster crew survived a fight and lived to report it, another two might not. There are no combat reports from the many hundreds of crews who did not get away.

Night-fighters often operated in pairs. One would attack while the other held off, waiting for the Lancaster's gun flashes to give away her exact position and attitude. Another trick was for an Me110, say, to hang about out of range with its lights on. While the bomber crew

---

* F/O Anstee is referring here to a nose-mounted searchlight, the RAF equivalent being the Havoc Turbinlite, disused after 1943.

were looking at that and wondering what it was up to, another fighter would attack from the other side. Rear gunner Norman Wells:

> 'One time, the second fighter was an FW190 and it came screaming past us ablaze from nose to tail. Somebody behind us had learned from experience.'

SECRET: No. 9 Squadron Combat Report

Unidentified T/E A/C passed across stern of Lancaster from starboard to port same height 300 yards range. RG opened fire when A/C was dead astern and fired two long bursts, tracer appeared to enter A/C. Fighter was not observed again as two scarecrow flares exploded close to the stern of the Lancaster and momentarily blinded the RG.
RG Sgt Robinson fired 600 rounds.

Scarecrow flares were, according to the Air Ministry, a German comedy weapon, a huge but harmless oil-filled flare which made a great flash but was nothing to worry about. It was only a daft German idea to try and frighten crews of incoming bombers, as if British bomber crews could be frightened by such a thing.

Scarecrow was an official myth. The reality was called *Schrägemusik*, music on the slant/angle. It was a method of attack from below at the unprotected belly of a Tommy bomber, using a pair of upward-firing 20mm cannon which were mounted behind the cockpit of a twin-engined aircraft and could be adjusted up to 72 degrees. The pilot fired them using a reflector sight in the cockpit roof and thus had much more flexibility in his attack than with the conventional method. Without Schrägemusik he would often still approach from below but would have to line up his aircraft with his target to fire his fixed guns, thus bringing himself into the bomber's field of fire. Thanks to an inventive sergeant armourer called Paul Mahle, the fighters could attack in secret and without danger to themselves.

The night-fighter pilot stalked his prey from below, trying to get directly beneath the bomber, in the blind spot and out of any slipstream turbulence. With the bomber crew oblivious to any danger, the pilot could take his time aiming. A volley of cannon shells into the fuel tanks or loaded bomb bay meant instantaneous and total destruction. The bomber blew up in the sky in a massive flash, leaving no evidence that an aircraft had ever been there and in one incident momentarily blinding Sergeant Robinson of No. 9 Squadron.

After a few fighters had got themselves too close to their bombers and gone up with them in the big bang, fighter crews started to ensure their own safety by firing from a little further away and aiming specifically at, say, the port inner engine (which ran the hydraulics for the gun turrets). They still achieved results but they were not always so spectacular. Rumours that Scarecrow flares were a Ministry cover-up were confirmed as bomber crews observed the curling coloured hoop of upward tracer and their colleagues going down by the more usual method – on fire and exploding on impact. Harry Irons:

'On one of my early trips, to the Ruhr, I said to the intelligence officer at interrogation that I'd seen fifteen of our bombers go down. "That's not right," he said. "Don't you go spreading rumours about bombers being shot down." I said I was just telling him what I saw. "What you saw," he said, "were decoys. Scarecrows." He gave me a right rucking. Well, I was only a sergeant and he was a flight loo. I had to agree with him.'

The majority of fighters were not equipped with Schrägemusik and for them the standard line of attack was from behind where, naturally, the Lancaster's sparse defences were concentrated. The rear gunner represented the biggest danger to the fighter and, therefore, the rear gunner was a prime target himself and was considered the crew member most likely to be killed or wounded, even if the aircraft was not shot down. Many did suffer, but so did the mid–uppers.

SECRET: No. 9 Squadron Combat Report
3/4 October 1943, raid on Kassel, P/O Walkup in WS/W.
Both gunners sighted FW190 at 700 yards, passing from starboard to port quarter. RG ordered prepare to corkscrew as FW190 lined up and turned to come in from dead astern. When E/A approx 600 yards, RG ordered corkscrew. Both gunners opened fire as did FW190 with cannon and machine guns. Cupola of MU shot away, also electrical and oxygen supplies to both turrets. MU gunner killed. FW came in again and opened fire at 300 yards, RG returning fire. Shots from RG entered E/A's engine. It turned sharply to port, rolled over onto its back and, when almost alongside our A/C at 100 yards, exploded. Pieces of the FW-190 hit our A/C and five members of crew saw this happen, therefore feel able to claim destroyed.

The mid–upper was Sergeant Angus Earl Leslie, 23-years-old, a married man from Romford. Rear gunner Sergeant Mullett was awarded an immediate DFM.

On the same raid, Flying Officer Comans, second time out, was attacked and had an engine catch fire. Nothing unusual in that, except for the cause of his trouble.

SECRET: No. 9 Squadron Combat Report
3/4 October 1943, Kassel. F/O J.V. Comans in WS/B.
Rear gunner noticed another Lancaster approaching at same height, 1000 yards, and informed pilot. The A/C closed to 400 yards and opened fire with two front guns, hitting starboard inner. RG ordered corkscrew to port, MU and RG opened fire and also hit one of the starboard engines of the attacker. As it broke away, burst was fired from its rear turret. MU Sgt Widdis, RG Sgt Bolland.

Chapter Three

The Lyon Months

While No. 9 Squadron lost more aircraft and crews – ten in April 1943, no survivors – and waited for new Lancasters to take the letter R and all the other letters, an Australian novitiate pilot, Sergeant James Lyon, had his second Dickies to Duisburg and Pilsen with Pilot Officer Boczar, a Canadian of legendary unhandsomeness and shortness.

'Second Dicky' was the term given to a new pilot's work experience, usually two trips as passenger with an experienced pilot – Dicky – and crew, sometimes only one when the pressure was extra high. The practice was generally stopped in mid-1944, although there were occasional instances thereafter.

Lyon got some idea of the circumstances of his new job when, on the bombing run at Duisburg, a flak shell exploded so close that it smashed the bomb aimer's Perspex, which would have made him jump had he been standing, as was probable, behind the pilot's seat. Next night, home from Pilsen with Boczar again, he heard that one of the squadron's crews had Failed To Return.

There was a nine night general break for the heavy bombers, coinciding with the full moon, the exception being the nineteen Lancasters of No. 617 Squadron setting out on the most famous raid of the war against the dams on 16 May.

Lyon's education continued with his first op as skipper, taking his crew – Sergeants Pack, Corkill, Jeffrey, Fielding, Denyer and Clegg – to Dortmund, when five of the squadron's seventeen Lancasters going contained new boys. No squadron losses that time, but another FTR on Lyon's next was at Düsseldorf, and on to Essen and a fresh month starting with five cancellations.

Lancaster Mark III EE136 arrived on squadron and was given the letter R for Robert. The Mark III was identical to the Mark I except for its engines, which were the Packard Merlins. These were originally built under licence by the Packard car maker for American airforce use, because the USAAF didn't have an engine with that sort of rating, but this arrangement was swiftly overtaken by the RAF's pressing need for Merlins – one for each Spitfire and Hurricane, four for each Lancaster – and Rolls-Royce, with their long tradition of hand-building, had not been able to mass produce, Detroit style.

So, Sergeant Lyon and crew on their fourth op, 11 June 1943, took the new WS/R to Düsseldorf. Nineteen Lancasters got away in what seems to have been fairly ragged fashion, with take-off times staggered between 2240 and 2355 hours and return times between 0319 and 0448 hours. Return times had many influences beyond the simple distance to fly, but half an hour was normally plenty for take-off for a score of Lancs. Lyon was one of the last to go and among the latest back, reporting 'an excellent concentration of fires' with a glow that could be seen 'crossing the Dutch coast homeward'. With smoke up to 15,000 feet, the general opinion was that it had been a good op – and, everybody had got home to say so, which was not the case for other squadrons.

Losses at Düsseldorf were forty-three – fourteen Lancasters, fourteen Wellingtons (10 per cent of those going), thirteen Halifaxes and two Stirlings; No. 12 Squadron had five Lancasters down with only three men surviving from thirty-five. Out of a massive force of almost 800 bombers, those numbers together represented about 5.5 per cent, which the strategists would say was not too bad considering forty square kilometres of the city centre was set alight, eighty or so factories were totally or partially wrecked and 140,000 people no longer had homes to go to.

WS/R-Robert was on the following night, for Bochum, and it lasted an hour and a half. Five minutes after take-off, the hydraulic pipe to the rear turret blew, making the turret u/s and forcing a return. The pilot had to fly on for a while to reach a safe place to jettison the bombs – nobody landed with a full load unless they absolutely had to – and came home soon after midnight. This was Pilot Officer John Evans, 20-years-old, on what would have been his tenth op had it counted, which, with his two second Dickies way back in April, made him an experienced skipper by the lights of the time.

DNCOs – Duty Not Carried Out – did not contribute to an airman's tour of ops, not even if the aborted flight had included hours over Germany, but for the aircraft it made no difference if the bombs were dropped on the target or not. It was still a flight, still an op, with all the work and tests necessary before and after.

Evans and his crew had had a very hairy time recently going for Wuppertal, when their Gee box got them off track and out of the bomber stream. Alone, they crossed the Rhine north of Düsseldorf, with all the searchlights and flak concentrated on them. They were hit, but spotted some red target indicators and fires on the ground away to starboard, so set off to bomb before realising that the aircraft was on fire. Evans ordered the incendiaries to be jettisoned, still hoping to drop his 4000lb cookie on Wuppertal, but the bomb aimer misunderstood and dropped the lot, so they flew unthreateningly over and through the town's defences and managed to get their machine home.

Not that their failure really mattered when the target, the Barmen side of Wuppertal, was almost obliterated, with four fifths of the buildings levelled in a smaller scale preview of the firestorms that would destroy much larger cities in the future.

R-Robert's second had been DNCO; the third proved more satisfactory with Sergeant Lyon and crew taking her to Oberhausen. There was ten-tenths cloud there, but sky-marking flares dropped by Pathfinder Mosquitos were accurate and the smallish, all-Lancaster force did a great deal of damage. That was at a cost, though, with seventeen Lancasters lost out of 197, mostly to night-fighters, among them WS/Q-Queenie captained by Pilot Officer John Evans.

Evans had not had a really settled crew. Changes in flight engineer and navigator particularly could interrupt that oneness so important to a bomber team. We can't know if that was a factor in the crew's deaths at Oberhausen, when a night-fighter sent them down to the banks of the Maas. Evans, aged twenty, still listed as sergeant, although recently made up to pilot officer, had three ancients in his team averaging thirty years old but not, on the night, his regular wireless operator Flight Sergeant Tom Myerscough, who had been in the crew that flew in EE136. He missed Oberhausen and instead had the news that all his mates had disappeared. He would last almost to the end of the year, to die on a Berlin raid on 22/23 November with 44 Squadron.

Replacing him at Oberhausen had been Walter 'Chap' Chapple, a man whose tour of ops was almost complete. While the rest of his old crew went off to safety, he had to find a couple of extra trips to cover for ones he'd missed through illness. This one would have made his thirty.

Sergeant James Henry Scott Lyon was variously known as Jimmy and Tiger, but generally as Benny, presumably after Ben Lyon the American film actor and, lately, radio star on the BBC Light Programme's 'Hi, Gang!'. R-Robert was never 'his' aircraft entirely, but he and his crew did eleven ops in her, so we can say R was more Benny Lyon's than anybody else's in those first few months.

He was kept busy enough after Oberhausen, but R had three weeks off, returning to duty on 8 July for Cologne. This city had been hit hard with several mass raids – Lyon had been there three times – but some of it was still standing so a Lancasters-only force was sent with half a dozen Oboe Mosquitos to mark.

Lyon was in EE136 WS/R, bombing from 20,000 feet and seeing two very large explosions. What he didn't see were any single-engined fighters weaving in among the bombers over the target, but they were there, as they had been on the previous Cologne run, and they were scoring. Bomber crews did not expect fighters where there were searchlights and flak, but this was a new tactic, later called *Wilde Sau*, wild boar. As well as the radar-directed two-seater fighters stalking their prey on the way in to the target and on the way home, these were single-seat opportunists who braved the defensive mayhem of the ack-ack gunners (who supposedly had agreed not to fire above a certain height), looking for Tommies caught in the searchlights, illuminated by the glow of fires, or silhouetted against the clouds, which they could attack with complete surprise and, therefore, with no fear of retaliation.

Being without airborne radar, the Me109s were, in a way, back to the earliest night-fighter times, searching without much hope for the sight of a bomber on a track and at a height they had no clue about – but the two-seaters and the ground controllers had the radar. The *Wilde Sau* could hang around in the sky where the Tommies were predicted, and wait for the two-seaters to show them exactly where to go with the falling torches of bombers they'd shot down.

At first, bombers suffering fighter damage over the target but surviving, complained of being fired on by their own, so sure were they that the Luftwaffe would not fly right over the action.

At Gelsenkirchen on 9 July, Benny Lyon and some of the other skippers saw the sky markers and bombed accordingly. The rest had to use a Gee fix with no markers visible, and the results were poor. The few markers that had been placed were ten miles out and other nearby parts of the Ruhr took more damage than Gelsenkirchen. Still, the population would have been pleased to know that, for a while at least, they would no longer be a target. The 'Battle of the Ruhr', apart from a few isolated thrusts, was over, with devastation wrought over all the major industrial centres. Bomber Command's attention would now be elsewhere. As C-in-C Arthur Harris put it, speaking of Krupp at Essen:

> 'By the end of July 1943, (Bomber Command) had reduced this great industrial complex to a veritable shadow of its former self (including) the largest single unit in the whole works, the huge Hindenburg Hall where locomotive production ceased and never restarted in spite of the fact that locomotive production then had equal priority with aircraft, tanks and submarines. Krupp also could make no more large shells, no more shell and bomb fuses, and gun output was cut by half.'

Something very similar could be said of the whole of the Ruhr.

The only squadron loss at Gelsenkirchen was from flak damage. The crippled aircraft struggled into France where the crew jumped for it, led by Canadian Sergeant John Duncan, thus beginning – for five of them – an epic escape (see *Luck of a Lancaster* by this author).

Noting that loss was Sergeant William Wrigley Watts Turnbull, pilot, of San Antonio, Texas and known, naturally enough, as Tex. His father, Elliott, had been born in Pueblo, Mexico, of English parents in 1880. The family moved to Texas when Elliott was ten and, by the time William Wrigley was that age, dad was a sales manager in the oil business. Wife Annie, born in Texas, also had English parents, so there were strong connections with the old country for the lad, youngest of three brothers, and that must have been a major part of his motivation to join the war. Like many Americans he enlisted in the Royal Canadian Air Force before his own country was attacked at Pearl Harbor and so was a true volunteer in every way.

Turnbull's first as skipper was Cologne on 8 July. Now he was off to Turin in Lancaster R, which was quite a contrast – a much longer journey, obviously, nine and a half hours minimum, and rather less danger from the local defences compared with the Ruhr. Searchlights and flak were disorganised, not what the Ruhr raiders were used to at all, and there didn't seem to be any Italian night-fighters to deter the bombers from wrecking the great Royal Arsenal and the Fiat works.

Death still lurked on the ways in and out. Tex and the others of No. 9 Squadron got home all right but fourteen crews did not, mostly 'lost without trace', which is to say probably shot down over the sea by German night-fighters operating from bases in the west of France and hitting the bombers as they wave-hopped across the Bay of Biscay.

Tex Turnbull was remarkably skeletal and the motherly WAAFs worried about him. Aileen Walker, a Nottingham girl aged eighteen at the time, worked in the officers mess where Sergeant Turnbull would soon be dining:

'That man, Turnbull, I did look after him. He was so, so thin and spoke so, so slowly. I'd go to him and ask him if he'd like some second helpings and he'd say no, he'd had quite sufficient, so we could never feed him up.

'One night I came off duty and there he was, leaning on my bike. I said, "what are you doing." He said, "I'm holding your bike for you. I'm going to walk you home". Well, he walked me home, he was blind drunk, and when he stumbled and fell I took my tie-pin off and held it ready in my hand. He had a certain reputation, did Tex Turnbull.'

The searchlights and flak seemed disorganised at Hamburg too, when EE136 WS/R went there on three of the four raids of Operation Gomorrah with three different crews. The destruction of Hamburg is well documented and described elsewhere. Here are reports from some of those who were there.

New pilot Sergeant Bill Siddle, who would become one of Lancaster R's most frequent drivers, was at Hamburg on a second Dicky and, two days later, as skipper of his own crew:

'There was a marked absence of fighters and the ground defences seemed to be in serious disarray, with searchlights waving aimlessly about the sky and the flak bursting in confused patterns well below the main concentration. We saw two aircraft shot down but from the lower echelons of Wellingtons and Stirlings, which must have meant the flak batteries were having to rely on visual sightings because of the effect Window was having on their equipment.'

Window was the radar countermeasure being used for the first time, strips of stout paper with reflective foil on one side which, dropped in 'clouds' from aircraft in planned sequences, confused German radar to such an extent as to render obsolete the night-fighter box system.

Another future R-Robert skipper had a quite different view, of a wild boar:

SECRET: No. 9 Squadron Combat Report
Date: 27/28 July 1943: Pos. Hamburg area: Lancaster 'L' Captain F/O Hadland

At the time of the attack the Lancaster was coned by approximately thirty to forty searchlights and was carrying out a diving turn to starboard to evade them. Both gunners simultaneously sighted an Me109 coming towards us from port quarter up, range 500 yards. Order was given to turn to port, but as pilot was already diving to starboard he continued this and tightened his turn. The E/A opened fire with a cannon in the nose and three machine guns in either wing. His opening shots hit the pipelines to the MU turret which was put out of action. The rear gunner opened fire with a good burst and some of his shots appeared to strike the fighter's starboard wing. The E/A continued firing until within 100 yards of the Lancaster when it dived to port bow and was not seen again. Considerable damage was done to the Lancaster's starboard elevator and numerous hits were scored on the machine. One cannon shell passed through a propellor blade of the starboard inner motor.

Tex Turnbull bombed as per briefing with the city well ablaze, and saw a pall of black smoke up to 15,000 feet. Other No. 9 Squadron crews reported the smoke at 18,000 feet and fires still visible from 175 miles away.

Ken Dagnall was bomb aimer with Flight Sergeant Jim McCubbin, future EE136 men:

> 'We were flying along and there was a Lanc right next to us. I said to Jim, "isn't that Fox?" Jim said, "By God, I think it is". It was really unusual to spot anyone from your own squadron on a night raid, much less actually know who it was. Anyway, we looked down at our instruments again and bang. Flak. Direct hit. And we knew who was in there.' (That was F/Lt Charles Fox and crew, no bodies ever found).

Siddle's rear gunner Clayton Moore, on the way home:

> 'From our high altitude as we drew near to The Wash, I could still see the fires that we had left raging through the streets of Hamburg, more than 300 miles distant.'

The final Hamburg raid was on the night of 2/3 August. From No. 9 Squadron's point of view, it was a mess. Most of the squadron took off on time but one was bogged down with a wheel off the tarmac and the three subsequently taking off late were recalled.

Pilot Officer Painter was skipper of EE136 R–Robert:

'No target attacked. Met severe icing, electrical storms and cloud up to 25,000 feet. Returned out to sea and made second attempt to run in. Same weather encountered so jettisoned load.'

Ken Painter and all his crew would soon transfer to Pathfinders with No. 97 Squadron. There were arguments for and against such a move. The work was even more dangerous, but a senior crew, thinking that a second tour of ops was likely, noted that such a tour with PFF was only fifteen. In Painter's case it was the 'even more dangerous' aspect that came uppermost. At Leipzig on 20 October 1943, two of his ex-9 Squadron crew parachuted out to end up in a POW camp; he and the others were killed.

Some of those on the last Hamburg raid did manage to bomb but it didn't matter. Losses had been well below the average and the city was a wreck. It had been a mighty blow at the enemy and a triumph for the Allies, and any opinion poll across German civilians and military would have shown a large majority in favour of surrender.

Harris was being proved right and the policy likewise. Germany's second city was hardly there anymore and most of the other industrial centres were rubble. If Britain had been the aggressor in 1939, the equivalent position would have been that the enemy she expected to conquer had instead flattened Birmingham, plus half or three quarters of Manchester, Preston, Leeds, Sheffield, Bradford, Hull, Middlesbrough, Nottingham, Leicester, Newcastle, Bristol, Southampton, Glasgow, Edinburgh, Aberdeen, Belfast, Cardiff, Swansea, Wolverhampton, Coventry, Stoke, Sunderland, Derby and

Liverpool, taken large bites out of every other large town and made a gigantic hole in the centre of the capital.

In between the Hamburg trips was a final stab into the Ruhr, at the hitherto forgotten steel town of Remscheid, not far from Düsseldorf – in fact, its proximity to that great target, also to Barmen and Wuppertal, had brought about its only war damage so far, being stray bombs meant for somewhere else. Remscheid was a kind of mini-Sheffield, 100,000 population making tools and other kinds of hardware, and on the night of its one and only raid it was reduced to a fifth of its former self by fewer than 300 bombers.

Benny Lyon was there, in R-Robert, and he thought the bombing to be rather scattered and falling short. It was not the usual crew, with Sergeant Chipperfield navigating, who would share in the good luck that WS/R mostly brought, and gunner Sergeant Houbert, who would not.

Eight Stirlings were lost in action at Remscheid, plus one crashed at home, out of the eighty-seven that were in the force. These disproportionate losses – against two Lancasters out of eighty-two, five Halifaxes out of ninety-five – were of course demoralising, and the Stirling would soon be withdrawn from Germany service, after the 22 November raid on Berlin when five out of fifty went down.

August 1943 would prove to be a busy month for Lancaster EE136 WS/R and the time when the famous nickname and nose paint of 'Spirit of Russia' were acquired. As was often the way with these identities, given in the hope that they would last and the knowledge that they probably would not, there is no hard evidence to show how or why this name was chosen. One theory is that Benny Lyon came up with it, looking for something with the letter R – as with WS/J Johnny Walker, WS/L Lonesome Lola and Lady in Red, WS/P Panic II – and deciding to honour, at a great distance, the fighting spirit of the Russian people. Bizarre as this might appear, it's as likely as any other story, vodka not being widely consumed in the officers mess.

Lyon took charge of R-Robert/Russia for an attack on Milan on 7 August, part of a major campaign to force Italy to capitulate as soon as possible. Mussolini had been ousted and imprisoned on 25 July; the Allies calculated rightly that there was no real enthusiasm for the war among the Italian people, which opinion their government could be made to share with some bombing raids.

The force was 195 Lancasters, going to Genoa, Turin and Milan; only one was lost in Italy, while another was found by a night-fighter on the way home across France.

Two nights later it was back to Germany, Mannheim, the great port and trading centre for the upper Rhine. Tex Turnbull took Lancaster R, with the itinerant gunner Sergeant Houbert in the back. He and the rest of the squadron encountered 'little opposition from the enemy defences' (ORB) and, probably due to the dumfounding effect Window was having, only seven Halifaxes and three Lancasters were lost out of 457 on the force, classified in those days as a medium raid.

A maximum raid on Mannheim just two years before, on 5 August 1941, had consisted of sixty-five Wellingtons and thirty-three Hampdens destroying a cigar factory, two paper works, a shoe warehouse, part of the railway station and ten houses. Tex and his medium-raid colleagues, although admitting to a scattered attack, started over 1,500 fires with total destruction or serious damage to more than 1,300 buildings.

Milan, famous for centuries for its art and music, was also an important trading hub and the chief industrial and financial centre of Italy. Elements of, as it were, Manchester, Birmingham and the City of London made it a golden target, and the biggest raid of all was 12 August, when 500 Lancasters and Halifaxes went. There were no losses at the target; two Halifaxes crashed in France, causes unknown, and one Lancaster had to be abandoned, also over France, with engine trouble. Tex Turnbull, in EE136, came back early with technical failures. The rest of the 500 did for Alfa-Romeo and a great deal more.

Tex and R set off again for Milan on 14 August with 140 Lancasters, one being caught by a German night-fighter over France. Next night, with Lyon in R, eight of 199 Lancasters were found out, mostly coming home from Milan. That was the last of the squadron's Italian raids, but there were twelve crews to go on 17 August, on one of the more controversial trips of the war, Peenemünde. This attack on a research establishment developing Hitler's war-winning secret weapons, the V1 flying bomb and the V2 rocket, is fully described elsewhere but it is worth restating the main points.

It was done in the full moon by almost 600 heavy bombers in three ten-minute waves, and would have been impossible to contemplate without a thoroughgoing spoof raid on Berlin by Mosquitos dropping marker flares and Window. This kept every night-fighter in the region over the capital for the duration of the raid, but it's only 115 miles (185k) from central Berlin to Peenemünde. The night-fighters could be there in twenty minutes. The German controllers kept their charges over the 'Big City' in great confusion, but not quite long enough to allow those bombing later to make their escape. About thirty night-fighters caught up with the tail of the force and shot down most of the forty-one aircraft lost on the night, almost 7 per cent, including twenty-nine of the third wave at 17.5 per cent.

The raid was remarkable in other ways too. Apart from a sixty-Lancaster special raid on Friedrichshafen (see following), it was the first use since the Dambusters of the master-bomber stratagem, whereby a single officer orchestrated the whole thing, judging the accuracy of marking and reordering as necessary, and bringing in the bombers when he was satisfied, and it was the first master-bomber raid altogether with a large and disparate force of Lancasters, Halifaxes and Stirlings from all parts of main force Bomber Command.

The German fighter crews could only wish they had been able to get there sooner. What a feast they would have had in the moonlight. Some of the Me110 crews had – for the first time – the options offered by the new piece of kit called Schrägermusik (see previous).

Peenemünde was classified as a success. Benny Lyon certainly thought so and, despite being in the third wave, No. 9 Squadron lost nobody. Two of the three aiming points had been obliterated and, thank goodness, they never had to go back there.

Tex Turnbull brought his EE136 score up to five with his last in that machine, to Leverkusen on 22 August, a fairly anonymous place on the edge of Cologne that was a main centre of the German chemicals industry. The factory complex of IG Farben (Bayer, Agfa, BASF) was the target. IG Farben was a massive organisation producing dyes, plastics, medicines, synthetic oil and much other stuff including Zyklon B, the pesticide adapted for use in killing people in gas chambers, and Leverkusen was only part of it.

It was a part that survived the raid intact. Five German workers were injured and one foreign worker killed at the factory, while four Leverkusen citizens also died and a dozen other towns reported damage, Düsseldorf the worst. There was thick cloud, the markers got it wrong, and most No. 9 Squadron captains bombed on ETA. Tex identified his position from the flak going up elsewhere, which he estimated to belong to Cologne and Bonn. On the bright side, only three Lancasters and two Halifaxes went down out of 462.

In the early years of the war, bomber crews had all the danger, but not much in the way of results, although they believed they were hitting their aiming points. In August 1943, with many advances in technology the early boys didn't have, great flocks of Lancasters, Halifaxes and Stirlings could still, sometimes, achieve very little.

On a cloudless but moonless night, 27 August, 674 four-engined bombers went to Nürnberg. Target marking was to be done by Pathfinder Lancasters using H2S, the airborne radar that displayed on a little screen a great deal of 'information', in the form of flecks and speckles revealed every few seconds by a rotating 'arm', somewhere among which was the profile of the ground being flown over. H2S was a complex and temperamental box of tricks but, unlike Gee and Oboe, it had no limit to its range. Against that, assuming it was still serviceable when the target was reached, a skilled, experienced and intuitive operator was needed to interpret the picture on his screen and find the aiming point in among the fuzz.

On this night, only the first Pathfinders could do their job accurately. As more and more aircraft joined the attack, the bombing crept back and the other PFF crews could do nothing because their H2S sets were u/s. Neither could the master bomber issue useful orders as only one in four of his command was receiving him.

Ken Dagnall, bomb aimer:

'The natural tendency was to bomb short. An eighth of an inch in your bombsight was half a mile or more on the ground and, being somewhat nervous while being shot at, your instincts told you to get rid of your bombs sooner rather than later. I perhaps went a little the other way, much to my skipper's annoyance. Generally, though, with bombing short, the result was that the bombing carpet tended to creep back. So they dropped the markers further up.'

The views of No. 9 Squadron, including Benny Lyon, now a Pilot Officer skippering EE136, were generally positive – good fires seen, results very promising, fires very numerous and concentrated on TIs. The squadron ORB states; '…there seems little doubt that the raid was very effective'.

The Bomber Command post mortem put most of the bombing in open country; German reports mentioned houses in the suburbs, and the zoo. Nothing industrial was hit, while eleven of each bomber type were lost to enemy action on this trip – that is, eleven out of 349 Lancasters, eleven out of 221 Halifaxes, and eleven out of 104 Stirlings – 4.9 per cent altogether.

Next up was Rheydt, a mixed-industry town of about 75,000 people near Mönchengladbach, which itself was also a target that night, 30 August. Both places were reduced by half in their first raid of the war. Recent arrival from OTU, Flying Officer English was skipper of EE136 on her twentieth. He'd second-Dickied at Leverkusen, skippered at Nürnberg, and here on his second trip he was introduced to the perils of prowlers. He reported not being able to see much, because 'cloud prevented observation of results on own target, plus pre-occupation with fighter'.

English and crew went to Berlin the following night in EE136 without any special excitement but, while R-Robert was off duty for a refit, they enlarged their experience of combat in the dark. At Hannover, they were attacked over the target by a single-engined aircraft which the 18-year-old mid-upper gunner, Derek Carlile, saw roll over and dive away to port, then, four minutes later, by a twin-engine, and an hour later by another twin-engine. The eagle-eyed gunners, Sergeants Carlile and William Hewitt, fired 1,300 rounds between them, and they had to be eagle-eyed because the fighter warning device, Boozer, showed nothing on every occasion, which was not really unusual. The following night at Mannheim, English's men got their own back, shooting down an Me109 that the flight engineer, Sergeant Mitchell, saw explode below them.

In mid-November, Flying Officer William English and crew, halfway through their tour with fifteen ops, would be posted as originals of the newly formed main force No. 630 Squadron at East Kirkby, where

English was boosted to Flight Lieutenant and the others, except engineer Norman Mitchell, were commissioned. Flying as an all-bar-one officer crew, with a second Dicky passenger on the Berlin raid of 15 February 1944, we can guess it was the fighters that got them in the end. They fell near Güstrow, on a line between Berlin and Rostock, the Baltic route, where flak would not have been dense but the fighters would be waiting. All died together; the body of rear gunner William Hewitt, aged twenty, was never found.

The third big attack on the 'Big City' in eleven days was 3 September. Lyon was in Spirit of Russia, along with a dozen others of the squadron and three hundred more, in a Lancasters-only force hopeful of reducing the percentage losses. It didn't work; twenty-two went down from enemy action, 7 per cent. Although No. 9 Squadron pilots generally reported clear marking and good bombing thereon – Benny Lyon saw smoke from the target up to 20,000 feet – much of the attack was wasted on rural ground and residential suburbs, although some important water and electricity works were disabled, plus a big brewery. The capital would have a pause now, before the full-scale Battle of Berlin began in all its horror.

The last of Lyon's operational tours was to Kassel on 22 October. He had all the same crew who had flown EE136 WS/R on her first op to Düsseldorf, except for a different rear gunner. Kassel was a hugely successful raid, destroying, broadly speaking, about two-thirds of the city, but losses were heavy – none from No. 9 Squadron – seventeen Lancasters and twenty-three Halifaxes directly from enemy action, plus three Lancasters and two Halifaxes crashing or otherwise finished at home, 8 per cent.

Lyon and the boys would have seen some going down, but they were back at beautiful Bardney with that indescribable feeling of relief that came with knowing so many who had not made it.

During the final stages of his training in Scotland, Benny Lyon had met a local lassie called Margaret Bruce and, once his tour of ops was complete, they married in November 1943. Flying Officer Lyon, DFC, was posted as a pilot instructor to 11 OTU, based at Westcott, Buckinghamshire, taking trainee crews on exercises in the twin-engined Wellington. He and his new wife settled into a rented cottage in the near-by village of Quainton, enjoying the less stressful, non-operational life but surely expecting a call to a second tour after a decent interval.

One such exercise, a night-time cross-country with a full crew, began for Flying Officer Lyon at 2005 hours on 15 March 1944, expecting a flight of two and a half hours. On that same night, a force of 863 bombers flew the long way round via the Swiss frontier to attack Stuttgart, hoping to wrong-foot the night-fighters, and a much smaller force of 140 Halifaxes and Stirlings went for the railways at Amiens. This was part of the plan to wreck transport in northern France so that the Germans would have great difficulty in bringing up reinforcements after the Allied invasion on D-Day.

The crew of one of the Amiens Stirlings, EH989 WP/P of No. 90 Squadron, were on their first op, three days after arriving on squadron, captained by an eighteen-year-old Mancunian, Flight Sergeant Joseph Spring, who somehow must have wangled his way onto pilot training when seriously under age. Three aircraft were shot down by flak near the target; the rest headed for home, job done.

Flight Sergeant Spring's wireless operator took a message to say they were diverted from home base at Tuddenham, Suffolk, to Westcott, which they reached at about 2230 hours, at the same time as Lyon's Wellington. Quite how they came to be at the same height while preparing to land is not known, but the Stirling bumped the Wellington from below and, severely damaged, flew on where it might. The Wellington, totally disabled, went in almost immediately at Quainton, killing everyone on board but, perhaps with last-second credit due to Flying Officer Lyon, missing the village and his own house.

After making a hopeless 'Darky' call for another place to land, the Stirling crashed at 2247 hours, seventeen miles away, also killing all the crew. 'Darky' was an emergency distress code word, mostly used when lost, or requiring urgently a place to land because of technical failure and/or flak/fighter damage. Darky calls were made on a special radio-telephone channel under the control of the pilot and were answered by any nearby RAF base.

The Air Accident Report looks nonsensical, blaming the Wellington crew for being off-track when they were almost home, and warning training aircraft not to fly in the vicinity of routes of the bomber stream, when the bomber in question had been re-routed and was alone. In any case, when bomber streams numbered hundreds, taking off from and returning to scores of airfields at night, and training aircraft likewise, and with communications fairly primitive, such a warning was worse than useless.

There is one final if-and-but to the story. The aircraft assigned to Lyon for this exercise could not be got ready in time and so he switched to another. According to the chiefy on duty that night, it would only have taken a few minutes to do the necessary to the original machine, but Lyon was not allowed to wait. Those few minutes might have made all the difference.

Benny Lyon's widow, Margaret, after barely four months of married life, went home to Scotland and there, at Coldstream in Berwickshire, their son Rowland James Lyon was born on 9 September.

Lyon's No. 9 Squadron bomb aimer and EE136 veteran, Harry Jeffery, DFM, had gone to 1661 Conversion Unit at Winthorpe as an instructor, where he had his six months off before a posting to Pathfinders, No. 97 Squadron. After several ops in May 1944, the squadron's machines were assigned – along with more than a thousand others – to pre D-Day raids along the French coast. Their target was also No. 9 Squadron's, the gun batteries on Pointe-du-Hoc, near the quiet little Normandy town of St Pierre-du-Mont, shown on the Operation Overlord map to be threatening the forces due to land at Omaha and Utah Beaches. Tomorrow, the US Rangers would be wading through waves and bullets, struggling up Omaha Beach and trying to take that same Pointe-du-Hoc promontory (portrayed in the 1962 film *The Longest Day*).

Ex No. 9 Squadron skipper Bob Lasham was also with No. 97 Squadron at St-Pierre. 'We had our briefing from our CO, Wing Commander Carter, DFC, and he told us about this target just on the French coast: "If you can call it a target", he said.'

The Wingco had every right to be confident and a little scathing. He could look at his crew and see three DFMs, a DFC and Bar, and a DFC, plus his own gong, owned by three flight lieutenants and a squadron leader (DFC and Bar in the rear turret). He had two bomb aimers with him; one was Flying Officer Henry Jeffery, DFM. Between them they'd seen and done all that could be, and they were shot down in the dark by a Focke Wulf 190. Lasham:

'Well, we lost two crews, including his and they never found any bodies from it. The rest of us were in and out in no time at all. We didn't know it was D-Day and we were flying home in the dark and the cloud but our bomb aimer called everybody back to see the H2S screen because it was showing the Channel full of ships.'

Chapter Four

How to Finish a Tour

Destined for posting to No. 9 Squadron as beginners was a crew led by Flight Sergeant Jim McCubbin, with bomb aimer Ken Dagnall – known as Joe – but they were reassigned at the last moment to Coastal Command, which was desperately short of crews to combat the U-boats in the Atlantic. Dagnall:

'I was just over eighteen. Jim would be twenty-two, a little older than most. We'd done OTU and instead of sending us to Lancaster finishing school they sent us to fly in Whitleys looking for submarines. That was a shocking aircraft, shocking. And to think people used to fly over Germany in them. We were going to fly over the Atlantic, not so dangerous, but we were liable to be attacked by Junkers 88s. There were squadrons based on the Atlantic coast at their equivalent of an OTU, and the learner pilots used to come out and try to find people like us. If they had done, it would have been Charlie Stewart's and my job to deal with it. So, while the Junkers was knocking hell out of us and Charlie was doing his best, alone in the rear turret of a slow-moving object with four machine guns, I was to wind myself down into the belly turret, grab hold of the Sten gun there and help him shoot the enemy down with that. Our plan, needless to say, was to escape into the clouds rather than fight.'

The Armstrong Whitworth Whitley, the 'flying barn door', compared favourably with the biplanes it replaced. It was a twin-engined monoplane with retractable undercarriage and enclosed manoeuvrable gun turrets; it was faster, carrying a bigger bomb load. However, matched against the new German defences it compared very unfavourably indeed. Designed in 1934, originally without flaps on the wings, but with angled wings to help take-off and landing, it flew with a unique nose-down attitude, as if searching the ground for targets. The first RAF machines to reach Berlin were Whitleys, dropping leaflets in October 1939 and, despite being already obsolete when the war began, some were still in Bomber Command service in the spring of 1942 before being switched to Coastal Command. One drawback noted by operational crews was its inability to carry on with just one engine, even with the Rolls-Royce Merlins that the later marks had.

McCubbin, Dagnall and co, went on their first sweep over the sea and never saw a thing. Next time out, 29 October 1942, proved exactly how shocking a Whitley could be. The navigator was Dr B.J. 'Bart' Sherry:

'Took off from St Eval at dawn for an anti-submarine sweep down The Bay (of Biscay). We set course from Bishop's Rock lighthouse on a twelve hour patrol, heavily laden with fuel and depth charges. We flew at between five and seven hundred feet through showers and squalls until around 1100 hours when Jimmy McCubbin, the skipper, discovered the port engine was leaking oil. At this point we were nearly five hundred miles from land. Jim decided to turn back to try and reach base before darkness. The wind, head-on during the trip out, now veered and was against us also on the return course. At 1500 hours the wind strength increased, visibility shut down and the sea was running with a heavy swell and breaking wave tops. With groundspeed reduced considerably, more serious trouble developed when the oil pressure in the leaking port engine dropped rapidly and the engine packed up. The feathering mechanism (in an ex-Training Command Whitley) was clapped out, so coarse pitch had to be selected and the propeller left to windmill, which reduced speed further.'

Ken Dagnall, the depth-charge aimer:

'We were going backwards. There was a terrific easterly gale, which was very rare. Our cruising speed was about seventy knots, but the wind was gusting up to a hundred and our navigator Bart Sherry, an Oxford PhD, said we weren't going to make land.'

Sherry:

'We were still a good hundred miles from the Scillies with a headwind rising to gale force. After jettisoning depth charges, guns and ammunition, the Whitley was only just staying in the air, wallowing along at thirty knots. Air Sea Rescue were advised of our position in case of ditching. We clawed our way back to forty miles off the Scillies when the starboard engine, which had been running alone and on full throttle, overheated and the engine temperature gauge shot into danger. Andy (Smith, w/op) transmitted our position with a final SOS and locked the Morse key on transmit.'

Dagnall:

'Jim said, "Ditching stations", which for me meant sitting against the main spar and acting as a relay for the skipper calling out our height, because without our intercoms plugged in, the rest couldn't hear him. "Hundred feet!", he shouted, and I shouted

"Hundred feet!" and hoped they could hear me. "Fifty feet!" and before I could get it out, a wave came up and hit us. I think that was the gentlest landing Jim ever made. So we got in the dinghy and watched the aircraft break in two and sink.'

Sherry:

'The starboard engine caught fire and seized. In a matter of seconds we hit the sea and, after the initial inrush of icy cold water, the dinghy was launched with all crew members aboard. The retaining cord was severed to allow us to drift downwind and clear as the aircraft sank. We were now exposed to the full force of the gale and started to ship water fast. Flying helmets were used to bale out the water and we were soon bitterly cold and exhausted.'

Dagnall:

'We sat with our feet carefully arranged between each other and settled down to wait for our rescue. We were well equipped. We had a Very pistol, a little compass, and we had a pigeon in case nobody had heard the wireless. Sherry wrote down the latitude and longitude and set the pigeon off with this vital information. Well, we'd ditched at about half past four on a late autumn afternoon. It was nearly dark and the waves were fifty and sixty feet high in a gale force wind blowing the opposite way to home. If we'd had a pigeon fancier among us he might have told us the bird had no chance of bringing about our salvation.

'Even if the pigeon had flown straight back through the night in record time, it might still have been too late. We didn't think to tie ourselves in until a wave broke on us and tipped us over.

Fortunately, we did all get back in and we made ourselves fast after that.'

Sherry:

'We were caught by an extra-large wave which overturned the dinghy and threw us into the sea. It floated upside down some twenty feet away and after a concerted effort we righted it and climbed back in, but it was a most exhausting process and we lost a lot of gear, although salvaging the emergency rations. Our priority now was to survive the night. I don't think we would have had the strength to deal with another dinghy capsize. So, cold and miserable, soaked to the skin, every muscle aching, we managed to keep ourselves going, alternately baling and pounding each other to keep warm. Around midnight we were heartened to see flares dropped by an aircraft and, rising on the crest of a wave, could distinguish a searchlight winking about a mile off. These welcome signs of rescue activity died away.'

As dawn broke at around 0600 hours, the crew felt that the wind had slackened a little and they might therefore have a chance of getting through their ordeal.
    Sherry:

'We checked the rations and the skipper started to get things organised. There were six pint tins of water, a clear graduated beaker, two tins of emergency rations – Horlicks tablets, barley sugar, chewing gum – a telescopic mast and flag, a first aid kit, two marine signals which proved useful as paddles but were little good otherwise, and two escape outfits. We decided to do without water that day and to start tomorrow at the rate of one pint tin divided between the six of us per day. Three Horlicks tablets per man per day was the basic ration.'

They would run out of everything by the time a week in the dinghy went by. Such a forecast was superfluous. If they weren't found sooner than that, they'd be dead anyway.

Sherry:

'We divided into watches of two, each pair on duty for two hours at a stretch sitting diametrically opposite each other. There was one wristwatch, my Service waterproof. As for the crew, Joe (Dagnall) and Andy were apparently quite complacent, Charlie was wearing his usual poker face while Jimmy had the McCubbin cheesed-off expression. Mac MacKenzie, the spare pilot (aged 19), was the big problem. We had only met him when he joined us shortly before take-off. He was very pessimistic about being rescued and became more depressed as time went on. After a while he refused to exercise to keep warm and even refused to converse.

'It was soon dusk and the wind had continued to freshen when, at about midnight, MacKenzie became restless, mumbling to himself. He sat up, struggling with the ration tin, trying to throw it overboard, shouting about setting the control column before the plane hit the sea. He was quite delirious and struggled furiously. It was all we could do to keep him and the ration container safely down in the dinghy. Finally, he quietened down and dozed off.'

It would be his last doze. Next morning was 31 October 1942. At dawn, everyone began to sit up and stretch except Mac, who lay back very white and drawn with his mouth open.

Dagnall:

'When he didn't respond to shaking we started to rub and slap him to get his circulation going but we had no effect. He was now quite cold with no heartbeat nor pulse. Dead. We slipped him overboard after removing his Mae West, identity tags and some personal items.'

The RAF issue dinghy was a circular inflatable with adequate room for three, or possibly four, but it was very cramped with six. Now they were five, and that they didn't quickly become four, three, or fewer, was a marvel in itself.

Dagnall.

'We only tipped over once more in four days, which was how long it took them to find us. If we'd been in some sort of a boat rather than the inflatable we'd have been smashed to pieces long before. As it was we rose up and down with the waves like a cork, sixty feet at a time, which was absolutely horrendous, like the very worst kind of fairground ride, but it saved us.

'A Liberator went over at one point but didn't see us or our two Very lights. If a German had seen us, in that sea, they wouldn't have been able to rescue us so they would have shot us. That was good practice. It stopped us getting back as trained aircrew ready to fly again. Yes, so they'd have knocked us off all right.'

Sherry:

'At 16.00 a plane appeared heading roughly in our direction which we identified as a Whitley. When almost abeam he turned towards us and circled. After three circuits he appeared to lose sight of us and drifted down wind. He did a square search and again missed us due to the broken nature of the sea. We took heart that the sighting would be reported and the search would continue. I was able to judge our course fairly well with the aid of the small escape compass, and announced that we were heading in the general direction of South America at a rate of two knots and into the area of anti-U-boat patrols, so our chances of being seen were improving.

'Next day, at about 09.00, Joe spotted another Whitley. We ran up the distress flag on the telescopic mast and waved it about. Just as we thought we had been missed again the aircraft altered course and headed towards us, marking our position with a smoke float and climbing up to transmit our position. At midday three Hudsons of Air Sea Rescue arrived, laid down a smoke float then dropped three yellow containers linked by a flotation line downwind across our drift path. The middle container burst open and a dinghy began to inflate, so we paddled to the flotation line and hauled ourselves along to the dinghy, which was the much larger Lindholme sort. The Hudsons departed leaving the Whitley standing by. We stored the other containers' supplies in the smaller dinghy and got into the Lindholme, which gave us more leg room. Apart from water, new rations consisted of more Horlicks tablets, another first aid kit, a pack of cards, a torch and, more importantly, a goose-down waterproof sleeping bag and two chemical hot water bottles. We bundled Charlie, now the weakest of us, into the sleeping bag and activated the bottles by filling them with sea water.

'About midnight it started to rain so we collected the rainwater into the dinghy canopy, drank it with great relish and settled down again to doze. Andy, who was on watch, wakened us and announced that he could hear a plane approaching. We had heard that some aircraft were fitted with radar capable of picking up a dinghy or a conning tower on the screen, and of course we knew that U-boat hunters had a Leigh light. They gave us a demonstration of their radar-guided accuracy as the plane approached and pinned us with a brilliant light first time. We were marked by a flame float and continued to be so marked every fifteen minutes. It was still dark when we became aware of an unusual shape on the horizon which resolved itself into the outline of a ship. Her searchlight homed in on us, followed by the rattle and smack of a boat hitting the water.'

Dagnall:

'We'd put all our belongings together in the pigeon tin, which was like a big biscuit tin, with over a hundred pounds in notes so it wouldn't get quite as saturated as ourselves. As we came alongside the rescue boat I stood up, which I thought I could do, holding the tin. But I collapsed and the tin went into the sea. "Bugger it", I said, which was the only comment made on the matter. None of the others said a dicky bird. In our state, material things meant absolutely nothing. Anyway, I got on board the ship and they laid me down on the steel deck and it was the most comfortable place in the world, and they gave me a big glass of something to drink. I was teetotal at that time and I didn't know what navy rum was.'

Sherry:

'I was woken at noon and in no time was tucking into a bowl of beef tea. The navy looked after us extremely well. We were aboard HMS *Cutty Sark*, a frigate, bound for Devonport. The captain, Commander Mack, looked in to see how I was getting on and I had a long chat with the ship's navigator, Lieutenant Maurice Green, whose bunk I was occupying. I gave him my flying boots as a memento and spent the time dozing and drinking until we docked at Devonport at 14.30. We had ditched thirty miles short of the Scillies and in three and a half days had drifted another hundred and ten miles to the south-west.'

Dagnall:

'I woke up in Dartmouth hospital. They had to get our legs back to normal. They'd been under freezing cold salt water for four days and we'd got a kind of trench foot.'

And so they came to No. 9 Squadron, the swimmers McCubbin, Sherry, Dagnall, Stewart and Smith, with the addition of Sergeant Norman Owen as flight engineer and Sergeant Percy Lynam, known as Dicky, in the mid-upper turret.

For McCubbin and the dinghy men, their first bombing trip – 2 April – was their fourth op, having done one and a double with Coastal Command. They were very kindly allowed to count the one that ended with four days in the sea, even though it had not been completed.

Dagnall:

'We went to Lorient. Three Lancasters, just three (and one of those came back early). It was a clear, moonlit night and the first time I'd ever flown so high. The old Whitley could only struggle up to 12,000 feet, and here we were in the top of the sky, millions of stars, and I thought if this is war, it's a picture. And the next night we were on for Essen, which, the grapevine said, was just about the most heavily defended place we could go to. Only Berlin was worse.

'Then we went to Kiel the following night, when our rear gunner Charlie Stewart shot off a few rounds at a fighter which apparently didn't want to fight.'

SECRET No. 9 Squadron Combat Report
Date: 4/5 April 1943: Pos. Hëide: Lancaster 'W': Captain Sgt McCubbin
Interception by an S/E E/A took place very shortly after bombing the target, Kiel. The pilot was carrying out continuous weaving at 21,000 feet. The E/A, believed to be an Me109, was seen 200 feet below and directly astern at 100 yards by the rear gunner (Sgt Stewart). He warned the captain who executed a diving turn to starboard while the rear gunner fired two three-second bursts at the E/A, the second of which was seen to hit. The fighter immediately dived away and disappeared while still at 100 yards range without opening fire.

No moon, visibility fairly good. Layer of 10/10 cloud at 6000 feet illuminated a little astern of our aircraft by searchlights.
Rear turret 450 rounds, no stoppages.

Ken Dagnall: 'That was three ops on the trot so they gave us a week's leave.'

The Škoda works at Pilsen (Plzeň, modern Czech Republic) had become much more important to the German war effort since Krupp at Essen had taken such a beating. Ken Dagnall took with him a little score to settle with his skipper:

'Going to Kiel a fortnight before, we'd run into a jet stream, which is like a tidal current in the air, and we'd been thrown off track and we were late. Skipper wanted to get on and get out when we found the place and my bombing photograph didn't look too good. Jim denied all responsibility, of course, and I'd had a bollocking from the CO. So I was absolutely determined that we'd hit that factory at Pilsen smack on, and I made him go round four or five times until I got the perfect shot. It was perfect, too. I was given a certificate, signed by Air Vice-Marshal Cochrane (OC 5 Group), to say that we'd hit the aiming point. I told the intelligence officer at the interrogation that there'd been a lot of smoke so we'd had to go around again.'

ORB, 15 June: 'The only flying was intensive bombing practice by five crews detailed for special ops shortly.'

Over the next two days there would be more practice for the said five, including the men led by McCubbin, now a Flight Sergeant. On 20 June they were briefed for Operation Bellicose. Their target was the Zeppelin sheds at Friedrichshafen, where the enemy was making radar sets, and it would be the first of a new kind of raid called shuttle: go, bomb, fly on, land far away, and hit somewhere else on the way back. In this case, far away was the north African base at Blida, on the coastal strip near Algiers, and somewhere else would be in Italy.

It had become apparent to a number of senior officers that conventional target marking could have its drawbacks, and the better you were at the job the worse the drawbacks became. If accurate dropping of markers was followed by accurate bombing, the markers could be blown out or become obscured by smoke, especially later in the raid. The 5 Group idea, called offset marking, was to mark a spot some distance from the target and do a timed run from that. This would work provided – as with any marking – the offset spot could be spotted. To help with all this, a raid manager was nominated, someone who would watch and direct not just his own squadron but all of the aircraft there. Friedrichshafen was the first instance of the master bomber technique since the Dambusters, and it worked to a certain extent.

Sixty Lancasters went, destroying about half of the factory's equipment plus some of the Maybach tank-engine works.

No. 9 Squadron had taken off around 2145 hours, bombed at about 0245 hours, and were landing in Algeria around 0745 hours. They had a couple of days off and hit La Spézia on the way home, Italy's chief naval base and a centre for manufacturing torpedoes and other naval armaments.

Dagnall:

> 'I was taken out of this world as we came back across the Alps. We were at something like 18,000 feet and it was a beautiful moonlight night, with a white ocean of cotton wool below, and sticking out of the cotton wool was the top of Mont Blanc. I couldn't help but watch it, on the port bow, until it vanished.'

Aileen Walker: 'We were waiting for them to come back and they were all carrying bunches of bananas. Nobody had seen a banana for years. They were like treasure.'

Some parts of Cologne were still standing so the squadron went there again on 8 July. Ken Dagnall:

> 'It was 10/10 cloud, couldn't see a thing, and it happened that we were in the first wave. The PFF hadn't turned up yet so there were no flares or TIs. We dropped on a Gee fix, which was very inaccurate. Our navigator, Sherry, told me on the intercom when we were there and that was it. What else were we supposed to do? Hang around all night at 21,000 feet circling over Cologne?'

At Nürnberg, bereft of ground instructions from Window-jammed radar, night-fighters were having to get in among the action over the target, whether they were designated wilde sau or not.

SECRET: No. 9 Squadron Combat Report
Date: 10/11 August 1943: Pos. Nürnberg Lancaster 'W': Captain Sgt McCubbin

As Lancaster was running up to bomb, a Ju88 attacked from the port quarter up. The rear gunner opened fire and told the pilot to commence diving to port. The Ju88 continued firing and shells hit the rear turret, rendering it u/s and injuring the rear gunner (Sgt Stewart). The mid-upper gunner (Sgt Lynam) had been killed, probably in the initial burst of fire from the fighter. The enemy aircraft then dived to port and took up position beneath the Lancaster approx. 600 feet below. It then continued to move from port to starboard and from starboard to port, and the front gunner (Sgt Dagnall) was able to get in several good bursts, the last of which brought sparks from the enemy aircraft which dived and disappeared below.

Dagnall:

'I was down, ready for bombing. There was no noise, no warning, you just saw it, a line of tracer going right through the aircraft, and it hit Dicky Lynam. On the intercom I heard him make his last sound, like a sort of breathy retching, and then this German fighter flashed past us. I should say he was a new boy, or not very experienced anyway. He'd overshot and he was looking round, wondering where we'd got to. I grabbed my (front) guns and blasted at him. Well, you've never seen such a hopeless mess. He was over there and my tracer was nowhere near. Jim had gone into the corkscrew, the fighter was swinging from side to side, and all those instructions we'd had about getting your target in the sights were a load of rubbish. I tried to imagine the fighter's flight path. I aimed for the sky where I hoped he would turn up, and he flew right through my bullets.'

As soon as he'd seen the tracer from the Junkers, Dagnall had pressed the bomb release, universally known as the tit, and scrambled for his gun turret, not realising that the release hadn't worked and the bombs had not gone. The attacks lasted eleven minutes with a full bomb bay. Dagnall hit the Ju88 on the starboard engine and watched thick black smoke pour from it as it vanished below:

'We were in a hell of a state. Everything was u/s for navigation and we found our way home by watching the defence boxes, the groups of searchlights and guns, and working out which city they belonged to. It was lucky for us that somebody flew over Paris, because when they opened up it wasn't anything like Germany and we could definitely tell where we were, and then Andy (Smith, w/op) said he'd got Tangmere. We threw everything out that we could, into the sea, including the bombs which were stuck and had to be released by hand, and we scraped in at Tangmere. I walked back through after we'd landed and saw Dicky. He was splattered all around the inside of the aircraft.'

The rear gunner, Charles Stewart, Arse-end Charlie as his crew-mates called him, was badly wounded in his legs and there was high activity getting him out. Ken Dagnall, back on terra firma, wasn't entirely himself:

'What we'd been through must have hit, because I was standing there in a daze. A ground crew flight sergeant came up to me and gave me my first taste of counselling. He belted me across the face and said, "Sergeant, get on with your job. You're all right." I felt so ashamed.'

Their Lancaster had got them home, but she was so badly cut about that she couldn't take off. She would mend, but not in time for going home, and the following night, back at Bardney, Dagnall learned something new:

'I was something of a loner, partly because I didn't smoke and I didn't drink, and partly because mathematics was my hobby. I used to take an algebra book with me on our ops. I saw very little of it but I used to take it. I'd signed the Sunshine Pledge and I kept to it, until Dicky was killed. When we got back from that I was off to do my usual routine for stress, which was to set myself a few mathematical problems from one of my books and bury myself in them, but Jim and the boys wouldn't let me. I had to go down the *Railway* with them, so in I went and ordered an orange squash. They said you're bloody well not having orange squash, so they laid me on a table and poured a double Scotch down my throat, after which I found life easier if I had what they gave me. So, for my first drinking session, apart from the navy rum on HMS *Cutty Sark* which I didn't taste, I had a minimum of eight large ones, and was I ill. I was sick during the night, what a mess, and I stuck to beer after that.'

Two replacement gunners had to be found. Flight Sergeant Houbert was the new mid upper. Dagnall:

'You had to get on with it. Here was somebody coming in for a dead friend, but you just did your job. So you're here for Dicky, you'd say. Well, I hope you bring us some luck.'

Ken Dagnall had had his counselling and the others had even less, but McCubbin, Owen, Dagnall, Sherry and Smith, with new team members Houbert and Elliott, would be going to Nürnberg again in a fortnight.

McCubbin and Sherry were now pilot officers, Dagnall and Smith were flight sergeants. The promotion board missed Norman Owen, so he was denied his extra one and sixpence a day (about £3 in today's money) flying on 3 September with 315 other Lancasters to Berlin. They saw one large explosion light up the sky for three seconds and bombed soon after from 20,000 feet. Berlin was the usual hell on earth; the Germans didn't get McCubbin but they felled twenty-two other Lancasters that night.

As the crew of Lancaster EE136 WS/R-Robert found out two days later, the extra hours spent in enemy airspace on these long-distance raids made fighter attack that much more likely. The crew was McCubbin's. He was on the last op of his tour, as were Sherry, Smith and Owen. Ken Dagnall had a couple more to do – he had the mumps to thank for one of them – and so the moods were mixed as they set off for Mannheim. Everything went to programme. Dagnall called 'bombs gone' at 2330 hours from 19,000 feet, and one minute later he called 'camera gone'. For the last time, almost a year after the four-day ordeal in the dinghy, five months after the first bombing trip with No. 9 Squadron, Jim McCubbin put his Lancaster into a climb and turned for home. It was half past eleven.

SECRET: No. 9 Squadron Combat Report
Date: 5/6 September 1943: Pos. Mannheim: Time 2332 hours: Height 20,000 ft: Target Mannheim: Lancaster 'R': Captain P/O McCubbin
S/E E/A sighted by RG (Sgt Elliott) following Lancaster. Pilot informed and Lancaster commenced to corkscrew. E/A closed on Lancaster from port quarter and RG opened up with a long burst at a range of 400 yards. E/A continued on a course to attack and broke away to port quarter after firing a long burst. MU (F/Sgt Houbert)

fired a few rounds only before being hit and took no further part in the combat. More attacks ensued, making five in all, firing long bursts in each attack and the Lancaster's RG also firing long bursts. During the final attack the E/A burst into flames as shots from the rear turret hit him. He dived beneath the starboard wing, obviously on fire, this was confirmed by the flight engineer and bomb aimer. This E/A is claimed as destroyed. No searchlights or flares were seen to be connected with this attack. The Lancaster suffered considerable damage, the bullet holes being too numerous to count.

MU gunner 20 rounds.

Rear gunner 3000 rounds.

With bullet holes too numerous, Jim McCubbin could look forward to a quiet-ish time at a training unit. They had bagged themselves a wild boar.

Ken Dagnall was looking for two trips as spare bod to fill in his quota. The CO said he'd take him. Fourteen went to Hannover. The Wingco bombed at the exceptional height of 22,000 feet and they came home to find foul weather and a hidden enemy over Bardney.

SECRET: No 9 Squadron Combat Report

Date: 27/28 Sept 1943: Time 0017 hours: Height 1,500ft: Location Bardney-Horncastle area: Lancaster 'O': Captain W/Cdr Burnett, DFC
As Lancaster approached Bardney outer circuit lights, with navigation lights on, an unseen aircraft attacked from port bow slightly below and opened fire with cannon and machine guns. Attacking aircraft was not seen by any member of the crew. The visibility was very bad at the time and it was raining heavily. Three engines were damaged and both mid-upper and rear turrets put out of action owing to severed pipelines, and there were numerous holes in the machine.

Wing Commander Burnett's aircraft, ED700 WS/O, was a particularly reliable machine even with numerous holes. Come December, on her fiftieth trip, she was to have a bad end, but this night she stayed faithful to Burnett. Also with numerous holes, three to be precise, but unaware of them, was Ken Dagnall, bomb aimer for the occasion:

'We were coming into the circuit when tracer flew across and the runway lights went off. Burnett got on the radio. "Put the bloody lights on," he said, "I'm coming in to land." Our starboard outer went, which was not too bad because we were circling clockwise, then the port inner went, and just as he turned in on the landing approach, the port outer packed in. There was no panic. He said, "Ambulance, fire engine ready," and touched down as the last engine stopped. He told them we needed dragging off the runway and said something about a pretty close thing, which I certainly agreed with, then I stood up and something started running down my leg. "Skip," I said, "I've been wounded," and he said, "All right," and that was that. Never saw him again. They gave him the DSO. He certainly could fly a Lancaster.

'The doc slammed me on the table and started poking around, no anaesthetic or anything, hole here, hole there, but he couldn't find any bullets or bits of shrapnel. He had this metal probe with a little ball on the end, which he pushed into my wounds. There was a nurse there so I couldn't say anything. They put a sticking plaster over each hole and I had a message to say I'd finished my tour.'

Ken would be an instructor for a year then he would join No. 227 Squadron. His skipper would be Wing Commander Balme, DSO,

DFC and Bar, a brilliant flyer who always put himself in the way of the worst jobs.

'He was an expert at the Immelmann Turn, a German World War One fighter manoeuvre. You were in your ten-foot-long Fokker Triplane and you found you had a Sopwith Camel on your tail. You did an instant half loop followed by a half roll and you were on his tail instead. Balme used to execute it in a Lancaster to get us out of a searchlight cone. They did say that when you were coned you had ten seconds to get out of it or you were dead.'

Chapter Five

The Road to Berlin

Full of hope and enthusiasm, disembarking at Greenock from the *Queen Elizabeth*, Cunard liner turned troopship, and transferring thence by rail to Bath Hill Court, a Bournemouth hotel turned holding barracks, a group of newly trained Canadian gunners looked with some surprise at their new country. One was Sergeant Clayton Moore, headed for a long career on No. 9 Squadron with skipper Bill Siddle and EE136 WS/R Spirit of Russia.

Having recently had his first experiences of flying and sailing, Moore now encountered civilian life on the southern English sea front in 1943:

'The golden sands were scarred by long coils of barbed wire and ugly concrete traps, while equally unattractive pill boxes and observation posts lined the cliffs overlooking the scene. On the beach there were no children playing; only the trappings of war. We had seen many indications of the conflict: the sunken ships in the approaches to the Clyde, the austerity and discomfort of our train journey south, the blackout, the shortages, rationing, the queues and the lack of fashion – few women wore stockings; many wore black arm bands. There were gaps in the street where houses and shops had once stood, replaced by large emergency water tanks. Windows were criss-crossed with adhesive tape and sandbags were everywhere. There was a marked absence of young men on the streets.'

Canadian aircrew were paid more than their RAF native colleagues. Americans like Tex Turnbull were counted as Canadians. The extra money was of limited use in a country where the beer was liable to run out before the session got properly started and commodities like cigarettes, nylon stockings and chocolate, taken for granted in Canada and the USA, had acquired high luxury status for the civilian population of wartime Britain. What scant quantities of these goods the ingenious transatlantic servicemen could glean and garner were reserved for that most deprived section of the populace, the young and pretty women.

Bill Siddle had his second Dicky on the first of the four Hamburgs, and took his crew on the next. They had three Hamburgs altogether, two Mannheims, a Nürnberg and a Rheydt, then Munich on 6 September, when they had a heavy flak shell explode very near, on the instant the camera operated, after dropping their bombs. Their Lancaster immediately went into an involuntary sideslip to starboard. Siddle got her back again but she was full of holes. Clayton Moore:

> 'As we flew westwards in the darkness I reflected on how we had fared. This was only our eighth op, yet it was the second time we had been clobbered by flak. During the same period, the squadron had lost five aircraft and crews, plus one on a training flight with all killed, plus a gunner killed (Sgt Lynam) and several injuries. These figures represented a chop rate of, roughly, a quarter of the squadron's strength in six weeks. I doubted seriously the chances of us managing to survive a complete tour.'

The flak had done more than make holes. One engine soon had to be feathered and at least one fuel tank had been emptied, but the damaged instruments didn't show it. A second engine packed up but started again. As they were on their approach, at 200 feet all three good engines stopped. A crash-landing was inevitable between Minting and Bardney.

The starboard wing hit a tree and the shock broke off the tail section of the fuselage, sending Clayton Moore and his turret spinning through the air before landing, guns down, in a field. The main part of the Lancaster ploughed on through various obstacles and finished up as a scrapheap. Every crew member was injured, some of them seriously, w/op Sergeant Culley only lightly, and they thought that Moore, spreadeagled and unconscious in his wrecked turret, was dead. He wasn't:

'Gradually, the nothingness gave way to faint, confused sounds. There were vaguely familiar objects in an unfamiliar setting. The landing approach. That was it. I was in a bomber. I was a tail gunner. We were going to crash. We must be down now. The feeble light of the dawn brought recognition. A cow was gazing into my turret with big, round questioning eyes, and I could see three men some way off, two standing, one on the ground. "When you've got a minute," I called out.'

ORB: 'On return, 'Y' (P/O Siddle and crew) ran short of petrol and crashed near the airfield. All the occupants, with the exception of the wireless operator, sustained injuries, which necessitated their removal to hospital.'

Siddle, Culley and Moore came back from their crash twelve days later and hung around for a while until a complete crew could be organised. They were ready to go by 18 October, when it so happened that the squadron's current record holder, Lancaster Mark III ED499 WS/X, with fifty-seven ops, needed to be air tested before going out that night in the charge of a novice. Let Siddle's men take her up, test her properly, and get their air-confidence back at the same time. The tests were fine and everything went to plan until they came in to land.

The memories of the crash proved too vivid for pilot Siddle, who pulled her up at the last minute after coming in too high and overshooting. After several more attempts the entire base was on alert, everybody was watching, and Wing Commander Burnett, the disciplinarian, was trying to talk Siddle down. On the ninth pass, they made it and the Wingco was on the R/T wanting the skipper in his office, now.

Siddle ignored the order and told his crew to become scarce except for the new flight engineer Jock Wilson, experienced but on his first flip with this pilot. He was to check the landing gear and climb back in, which he did, along with his new skipper. After three more take-offs, circuits and landings, Siddle was satisfied that his demons had been exorcised, although he knew that the satisfaction was likely to be purely personal and of no further interest to the RAF. He was in for a court martial, that was sure and, in easier circumstances, such would have been inevitable. In a war, and in especially difficult times in a war, the Wingco could not afford to lose a good pilot. After a thorough, fully embellished Burnett-style rollicking, Siddle was given one more chance provided he could find a crew willing to go up with him.

Hannover that night was a very shaky do, with nineteen lost in an all-Lancaster raid of 360, at that time the highest number to go. One of those nineteen was the 5000th bomber loss of the war; one was ED499 WS/X, flight tested and given a record number of circuits and near-bumps by Siddle. The captain was Canadian Pilot Officer Howard Gould on his first trip, shot down half a dozen miles from Hannover, all crew killed.

Siddle, Culley and Moore, with four replacements, flew to Kassel on 22 October, seven weeks or so after their crash. Their regular mid-upper, Sergeant Dicky Jones, also came back to Bardney, was assigned for his restart to the experienced Pilot Officer Ken Warwick (aged twenty) as a fill-in to Berlin. Jumped by a fighter a few miles from home, they tried to get in at Gamston but crashed there. Dicky Jones, Warwick and three others were killed.

Siddle and his luckier lads carried on towards their first date with EE136. Clayton Moore had the cost of flying goggles and a boot, lost in the crash, deducted from his pay.

Our heroine aircraft had also had some time off for a refit, and returned for Siddle and a target in southern France, Modane, in an Alpine valley between Grenoble and Turin, where German troop trains were assembling in the marshalling yards and the railway for Italy went into a tunnel. Crews flying down the valley on 10 November could see the trains and men running for shelter, but there was not much shelter to be had and there was no opposition at the target. The railways were severely smashed about. This was a remarkable raid, a bombing success in which, out of 300+ Lancasters, not one was lost.

Just as Göring's and Hitler's preoccupation with London had cost them their advantage early in the war, so Harris's with Berlin. The 'Big City' was formidably well defended and it was widely spread out, its streets not suitably arranged for a Hamburg firestorm. It was a long way for machine and men and, no matter how the routes were varied, the Germans would not have too much trouble guessing the destination of the bomber stream. The use of Window had made the old cell system obsolete, so new and better tactics were developed for the night-fighters. On these longer journeys the slower and lower flying Stirlings and early marks of Halifax suffered terrible losses. Squadrons flying these aircraft had to be withdrawn before they ceased to exist.

The Battle of Berlin is said to have run from 18 November 1943 to 31 March 1944, when Harris was forced to desist by the need to soften up targets closer to home, ready for the D-Day invasion. He and others believed that there could be no war, no German resistance, if there were no Berlin. They knew it would be hard beyond anything Bomber Command had done before, but it would be worth it if it stopped the fighting. The main struggle was up to the end of January, by which time the night-fighters were having a wonderful run, and Bomber Command, out of range for Oboe target marking, was in danger of spiritual fragmentation. Aircrew could see their bombing was poor. If the marking was scattered, so was the attack. In fact, they were inflicting more damage than it looked from 22,000 feet, but the big fires and high smoke and vivid explosions did not seem to compensate for the many, many flaming torches falling to earth.

The torches did not include EE136 despite twelve opportunities, starting with 18 November and captain, Pilot Officer Blow.

Harry Blow had second Dickied with Tex Turnbull to Kassel on 22 October. He'd led his crew to Düsseldorf, Modane, and now the 'Big City'. On that significant afternoon, seventeen crews of No. 9 Squadron were briefed to take off around half past five for the long haul. The Berlin force was 440 Lancasters, sixty more than had gone to one target before, and four Mosquitos, finding their way across the northern Dutch coast and on between Bremen and Hannover. A major second raid was mounted on Mannheim with a similar number of Lancasters, Halifaxes and Stirlings to be treated to the defences of the Ruhr. The bomber streams flew into enemy territory at the same time but 250 miles apart.

The weather men had said clear tonight but they were wrong. At Berlin, bombs fell in many parts of the city but there were no concentrations; some factories were hit, and some houses. Harry Blow, in the Spirit of Russia, bombed on this raid with both mid-upper and rear turrets u/s. He was a Lincolnshire farmer, a no-nonsense, press-on type, and Pilot Officer Mick Maguire, squadron armaments officer, knew him well:

'One time I was in the billet, a Nissen hut I shared with Harry Blow, when he came in. "Hello Harry," I said, "what are you doing here? You're on leave." He ignored what I said. "What's happening tonight?" he wanted to know. "What's the target?" I hadn't been told. "What's the bomb load? What's the fuel load?" You could guess the target with that information, or at least the kind of target. "Any aircraft going spare?" I said, "Harry, you're on leave." He was quite a fierce little fellow. He came right up to me and said, "How do you think I feel, on leave, when the bomber force is going over my head at night? I can't stay home. I'll rake up a spare crew." "Your own crew will love you for that," I told him. And he wasn't the only one who did that sort of thing.'

Blow would fly a round dozen to Berlin and come home twice with a fin bent at right angles after a mid-air collision. He would have a wing badly damaged by a bomb falling from above. He would be shot up by a fighter with 30mm Mauser cannon, luckily fired at low velocity or the shells would have exploded when they lodged inside his fuel tank. All this happened to Harry Blow and his long suffering crew, but none of it was considered worthy of mention in the ORB.

Pilot Officer Bill Chambers took WS/R to Berlin next, 22 November, one of 753 heavies and the last time Stirlings were sent to Germany. The weather was foul, which made accurate bombing difficult, but also kept the fighters at home. Aiming the bombs for Chambers was an American, USAAF Technical Sergeant James John Hannon, from the Bronx, New York, working on sky markers in ten-tenths cloud and helping to make this raid the most destructive of the war. To add to the effectiveness of such an attack, Harris would point out the great numbers of able-bodied men kept back for home defence. In this case he could have added 50,000 soldiers drafted in to help clear up the damage.

That was Chambers's only flight in WS/R. By the end of February, he was around two-thirds through his tour when he and his EE136 crew, with one difference, flew in another long-server, ED654 WS/N 'Cutty Sark', sixty-two operations, to Stuttgart. Only seven Lancasters out of 460 were lost during the attack due to a large diversionary exercise over the North Sea by training flights and a feint attack on Munich, and the Bosch factory took several very effective hits. Two of the lost Lancasters were from No. 9 Squadron, one with a crew on their second op, one the experienced Chambers team. They fell near Welzheim, about 20 miles south-east of the target.

Withdrawing the Stirling from German service had left Harris eleven squadrons shorter. The Americans wouldn't help by going to Berlin during the day, so the Battle of Berlin was looking ever, ever harder. Flying Officer James Ling was given the next two Berlins in EE136 on 23 and 26 November. He'd been on squadron for a month, having second Dickied on Benny Lyon's penultimate on 20 October to Leipzig. Soon after take-off for Berlin on 23 October, oil pressure on the port inner dropped and the engine overheated – 'temperature went off the dial' – so they had to jettison and come home, so they missed a raid with over 5 per cent losses.

This raid and the next illustrated the increasing complexity of the job. Every time one side found an advantage, the other side countered it. The RAF was broadcasting fake instructions to the night-fighters, so the Germans introduced a female commentator, so the RAF immediately brought in their own woman who ordered the German pilots home or they would be unable to land in the fog. The Germans were using parachute flares dropped by fighters to light up the bombers; RAF Mosquitos dropped exactly similar flares well away from the bomber stream to attract the fighters' attention.

On 26 October, the main raid was just under 450 Lancasters going for Berlin, while almost 180 bombers, mostly Halifaxes, went for Stuttgart. The two forces flew together to Frankfurt, which the Germans assumed was the target; then split, so neither force had much fighter intervention outward bound. On the way home, however, with the Germans wise to events, losses grew. There were few fighters over the capital, but the many ready to defend Frankfurt had time to readjust and pick up on those who strayed off track on the way back.

Counted as lost to enemy action were twenty-eight Lancasters, while, remarkably, half as many again crashed at home, mostly damaged by flak or fighter – 10 per cent all told and the worst so far. Ling, in EE136, thought he'd hit the target and noted massive fires, but the markers were some six miles out. Even so, Berlin was indeed a big city and many buildings were destroyed, many factories and, over the three nights, approaching half a million people lost their homes.

Ling was there again on 2 December, and he had seven more Berlins to come, a total only exceeded in No. 9 Squadron by Harry Blow's twelve. After the moon lay-off, James Ling was reunited with EE136 for Frankfurt on 20 December. There was a lot of fighter activity on this one – Ling missed it – one No. 9 Squadron Lancaster was 'riddled from stem to stern' but got home with no casualties, another had to ditch off Great Yarmouth with a dead rear gunner, and fifteen more went down, also twenty-six Halifaxes, including one hit by bombs from above, plus two crashed at home.

Cloud and German decoys – fires and dummy TIs – had given the PFF too many puzzles. The marking was poor and, for a 7 per cent loss, the damage was mostly 'civilian' – houses, schools, the cathedral – with nothing destroyed that would much hinder the war effort.

For EE136's thirtieth on 23 December, Bill Siddle came aboard again for his first Berlin, with a fill-in navigator, Flying Officer James Hearn, who was in for an exciting night, but already knew how close one could get to the chop, having been wounded in fighter attacks at Kassel that killed the mid-upper gunner and disabled the rear gunner.

James White Hearn would fly most of a tour before dying with his regular crew in March.

Siddle's rear gunner, as usual, was Clayton Moore:

'Berlin was looked upon by most crews as the ultimate test of nerve and skill. A trip to Essen or Cologne usually lasted little more than four hours, of which about ninety minutes was in enemy air space. Berlin demanded long hours of concentration, alertness, and suffering severe cold. In addition to the heated reception we could expect from the city's considerable defences, there was the guarantee that the fighters would be in close attendance for most of the six hours spent over Germany and Occupied Europe.'

Fifteen Lancasters went down on route. Two more collided over Lincolnshire, all killed, and it was very nearly the end for EE136 too. As Siddle turned away after bombing, a Lancaster was hit only a few hundred feet away and, fatally wounded, headed for WS/R. Siddle put his aircraft into a hard dive to port while yelling for instructions from his rear gunner. Which way should he go? Moore:

'I watched and waited, unable to decide. The doomed aircraft was out of control with the port wing blazing furiously, a large section of the fuselage also in flames, and it was right behind us and getting closer. It began to break up about a hundred yards astern. "Level out to starboard, now," I shouted. I thought I'd detected a slight swerve to port in the dying bomber. As I spoke, the fire flared in the after part of the fuselage. I could clearly see two figures silhouetted, trying to get out. As Bill pulled us up out of our dive I strained against the G forces to watch the wretched Lancaster. The port wing broke free and the fire spread to the starboard side as it went down and down in a drunken slow spin. I didn't see any parachutes

Where lies the luck – with aircraft, or crew, or letter? The second Lancaster WS/R, ED308, flew four ops, all with Sergeant T. Doolan and crew, but was hit on the fourth, killing the rear gunner. The next, WS/R, ED501, flew seventeen ops in February to April 1943, eleven of them with Doolan and new gunner Harry Irons, until the squadron commander failed to bring her home. Here we see the lucky crew with ED501; captain Doolan is third from right; gunner Irons third from left.

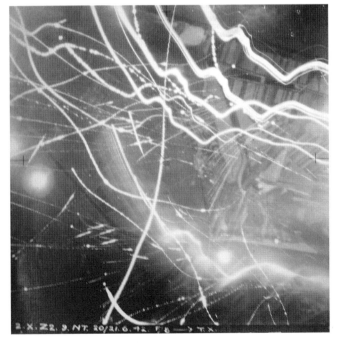

Harry Irons on his first op: 'So off we went to Düsseldorf and I'd never been so frightened in my life. I didn't know what was going on. I couldn't credit the flak and the searchlights and all the aircraft blowing up. I had the best view from my turret. I was in a daze when we got back. But you did get used to it.' This particular flak and searchlights was over Emden, and you had to get used to it because it was the same everywhere you went in Germany.

The first of forty-two crews to fly in Lancaster EE136 were, left to right, back row: Sergeant G. Clegg, rear gunner; Flight Sergeant J.H. Lyon, pilot; Sergeant H.W.E. Jeffery, bomb aimer; Sergeant A. Fielding, wireless operator. Front row: Sergeant A.G. Denyer, mid-upper gunner; Sergeant R.W. Corkill, navigator; Sergeant K. Pack, flight engineer. Plus Whisky the dog.

The organised chaos of assembly for a big raid is shown here, as No. 9 Squadron crews wait for their lifts out to their aircraft before setting off for Hamburg as part of Operation Gomorrah.

Sergeant C. Payne and crew took EE136 to Hamburg on 29 July, on the third of the four Gomorrah raids. They are seen here with W5011 WS/Z, thirty-nine ops between June and November 1943, a career that ended on 18 November after returning early from a Berlin trip with sick crew, only to have an engine fail on landing and be forced into a write-off belly-flop. Sergeant Payne and all his men had the luck to last the whole way through.

Tex Turnbull, the American volunteer pilot, flew five operations in EE136. Flak and searchlights like this – seen by him over Berlin in September 1943 – were all in a night's work for these men. They knew they were going to meet it every time.

This picture shows the flak over Mannheim, taken from Tex Turnbull's Lancaster on the night of 23/24 September 1943. He'd been there before, in EE136, on 9 August when, we can be sure, the flak was just as bad.

Leaflet dropping was considered – by those who ordered it – a form of psychological/political warfare, intended to undermine German morale and increase 'restlessness', as they put it, in France, The Netherlands and the other Occupied Countries. What the postmen thought of it, for whom delivering leaflets was every bit as dangerous as delivering bombs, can easily be imagined. They knew that, regardless of the potential effect of the message, leaflets dropped from 20,000 feet would be scattered by the wind far away from their intended targets unless let go in a package, in which case a bomb would have been better. Churchill's statement offers life in freedom and happiness in return for unconditional surrender. The later one, showing bomb totals, does not show leaflet totals; Bomber Command had already dropped 250 million by mid-1942.

Wing Commander Pat Burnett, DSO, DFC (right) was CO of No. 9 Squadron from April to November 1943, with a reputation as a disciplinarian. In the September, his homecoming Lancaster was shot up by a night-fighter and he landed with no engines, with wounded bomb aimer Ken Dagnall on his last trip. On 18 October, he had to talk down pilot Bill Siddle, who had lost his nerve in a crash and was failing again and again to land on all four engines.

One can hardly imagine a more inappropriate exercise than this one, for Jim McCubbin, Ken Dagnall and co, considering most of them had already survived four days and nights in a dinghy in the real sea. The captain of the ship, seated facing the camera, clearly has what his navigator called his cheesed-off expression.

ED499 WS/X was the No. 9 Squadron record holder for a while. Here she is with her most frequent flyers, Flight Lieutenant G.F. 'Robbie' Robertson and crew, after a trip to Cologne, her thirty-third. The name Panic II was awarded by Robertson and, by virtue of his Portuguese childhood, a painted proverb in that language which translates as 'God looks after drunks and little children'. ED499 was lucky enough for Robbie, seeing him out of his completed tour, and going on to achieve fifty-seven ops before being flight-tested and given a record number of circuits and near-bumps by EE136 stalwart Bill Siddle. She then went on her fifty-eighth with a first-time crew and never came back.

EE136 went to Berlin, her thirty-eighth op, captained by Pilot Officer Mathers, on the night of 28/29 January 1944. It was cloudy and much of the bombing was done on sky-markers. Mathers saw one big explosion and thought the area to the north-west of the target was burning best. In fact, Hitler's newly built Chancellery (above) was among the wreckage – 'mountains of it', according to the official German report.

Flying Officer Harry Forrest, DFC – as he was when he finished – took EE136 to Schweinfurt and Stuttgart in February and March 1944, with no special incidents to report. In another Lancaster over Nürnberg, his mid-upper gunner was killed, but he and all his EE136 crewmen saw out the war. Forrest stands fifth from the left in this shot of aircrew and ground crew together.

Flying Officer James 'Benny' Lyon, DFC, after surviving all the many dangers of a tour of thirty bomber operations, including eleven in Lancaster EE136 WS/R, was killed on the night of 15 March 1944 in a training accident. The Wellington he was flying as instructor/pilot collided, during landing approach, with a Stirling that was returning from a mission in France.

The photograph was taken in July 1944, when this crew flew in EE136 WS/R. After a summer of good luck, they went to the aqueduct at Münster with a Tallboy bomb and were shot down on the way home, probably by a night-fighter, over Gelderland, when all were killed except for the bomb aimer, who was taken prisoner of war. Back row left to right is Sergeant Jack Simkin, flight engineer; Flight Sergeant Louis Harding, navigator; Flight Sergeant L.W. Langley, bomb aimer; Sergeant Leslie Hambly, rear gunner. Front row: Sergeant Maurice Hayward, wireless operator; Pilot Officer (later Flight Lieutenant) Charles Scott, pilot; Sergeant Frank Saunders, mid-upper gunner.

ORB: *31st July. Ten aircraft (of No. 9 Squadron) attacked Joigny La Roche and concentrated bombing was carried out. The whole target area appeared to be hit.* As we can see from the photograph it certainly appeared so – and was so. The railways were wrecked. The photographer was Flying Officer 'Lucky' Adams' bomb aimer, Sergeant Jackson, whose flight in EE136 was yet to come. At Joigny, WS/R was skippered by Flying Officer Tweddle.

Trossy-St-Maximim was a flying-bomb storage site, attacked by about 200 Lancasters and in some disorder, judging by the complaints from crews about jostling and indiscipline. Five Lancasters went down, at least one hit by falling bombs and two more colliding. Photograph by Flying Officer Tweddle's bomb aimer, Sergeant Singer, who had been in EE136 at Joigny.

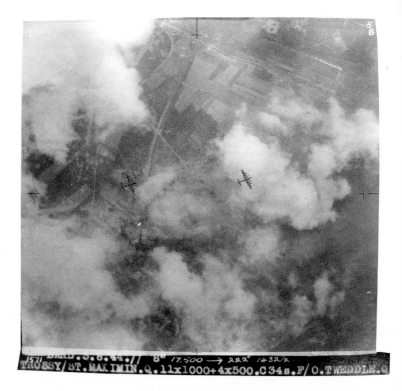

Flight Sergeant S.F. Bradford took his crew on their first op, La Pallice, in EE136, and flew one more to Ijmuiden, where this picture was taken by his bomb aimer, Flying Officer Owen Hull. Bradford was then promoted to pilot officer and posted to Coastal Command at Eastchurch, and his whole crew were taken over by Flying Officer Ernie Redfern with, eventually, fatal results. Photograph shows the E-boat pens being attacked.

Flying Officer Roy Lake took off for the first of the three *Tirpitz* raids by Nos. 9 and 617 Squadrons on 11 September 1944, the one due to land in Russia, but his Tallboy bomb came loose in the bomb bay of EE136 WS/R 'Spirit of Russia' and he had to turn back. Pictured here is a Tallboy, with armaments officer Mick Maguire looking in from the right. This bomb was the biggest thing that could possibly fit inside a Lancaster.

Four captains of EE136 WS/R in one picture. Most frequent flyer Roy 'Puddle' Lake is standing third from right, with Les Keeley last on right. In the front are (left) Ron Adams and Doug Tweddle.

Flight Lieutenant Charles Scott, as a rookie pilot officer, had skippered WS/R twice in July. By 23 September he had clocked up twenty-eight ops and the rest of the crew were on twenty-seven, which was when they were all killed in their crash in central Netherlands, about 70 miles from the coast. On 23 October, navigator Curly Harding's wife gave birth to son Michael, who became the well-known entertainer. Sergeant Jim Brookbank was a recently arrived bomb aimer with another pilot called Scott: 'We were posted as killed instead of Flight Lieutenant C.B. Scott's crew. When the Service Police came to clear up our quarters and started taking our stuff, it was a stroke of luck that some of us 'dead' men were there, or the telegrams would surely have gone out to the wrong crew's families.' Sergeant Brookbank poses here with a Tallboy bomb standing on the right.

The American pilot Ed Stowell had only one op in EE136, but he was lucky enough to complete the rest of his tour.

Now with No. 189 Squadron, EE136 CA/R was captained by Flight Lieutenant Fred Abbott, 4 December 1944, to Heilbronn. The bombers started a firestorm that completely destroyed the city centre and surrounding districts. The official estimate was four-fifths of the town laid waste. Thousands died in the fires, half the population fled, and Heilbronn was, as we can see from the picture, no more.

This is the Urft dam as it was when built in the early 1900s. Flying Officer Seddon flew EE136 to it on her 100th operation and, in common with the other 204 Lancasters on the trip, left it pretty much as you can see it here.

Flying Officer Clifford Newton, of Rosewood, Michigan, flew his second operation in EE136, to the U-boat pens at La Pallice on 16 August 1944. His luck lasted through the rest of the year and many adventures, including a shoot-out with two E-boats after the third *Tirpitz* raid, but ice in his fuel produced a fatal crash on a bitterly cold New Year's morning, 1945, flying the latest WS/R replacement for EE136. He was known as a quiet fellow but here he has been volunteered to pose for a press picture, explaining how they sank the *Tirpitz*.

Flying Officer Sidney Reid of No. 189 Squadron captained EE136 on her 104th op to Royan, a German-held town on the Atlantic coast, a pocket of strategic importance in otherwise liberated France. It was a devastating daylight double-wave raid, as the picture shows. Among the few losses were the ex-EE136 crew led by Flying Officer Jack Coad.

With the war nearing its end, crews could calmly view in daylight the devastation they'd caused at night, among searchlights, flak and fighters. An ex-EE136 skipper took this picture over Bremen in March 1945.

Sad end indeed, as a fire-fighting exercise, but one must not get sentimental about a heap of old iron, surplus to requirements. The first hundred ops are clearly shown; the next nine are partly behind the shoulder of the airman on the right.

come out and I watched it strike the ground far below us. You only have two thoughts when you see something like that. Poor sods, and by Christ it could have been me.'

Six nights later, with Christmas in between, they were there again, Siddle, crew, and EE136, with an Australian second Dicky, Flight Sergeant Colin Peak, who would himself become an EE136 partner in the New Year. This was another in a series of ineffective raids, with cloud cover resulting in poor marking and most of the bombs falling where they could do little damage. For a change, losses were not so great either, 3 per cent of a big force of 700+, when 7 per cent was becoming the norm.

Happy New Year everyone. In 1943, No. 9 Squadron had lost fifty-five Lancasters on ops and four more in accidents. Bomber Command had lost 1,117 Lancasters, 883 Halifaxes, 418 Stirlings, 327 Wellingtons, sixty-seven Mosquitos, twenty Whitleys and fifty-four of other types on ops, 2,886 aircraft altogether, plus another 231 in accidents, plus another 764, mostly Wellingtons and Halifaxes, in training at OTUs and Conversion Units.

The devastation wrought by Bomber Command in 1943, in the Ruhr, at Hamburg, and elsewhere, was beyond anything seen in the world before, and had made the defeat of Germany, by bombing alone, look a realistic possibility. The switch to Berlin was proving to be a mistake. Losses were great, damage done was not in any kind of proportion, and keeping up morale among the crews was perhaps an aspect of the job that had not been properly considered.

The first op of 1944 was Berlin again; this time, EE136 was in the charge of new boy, Pilot Officer Ron Mathers, who had second Dickied with Tex Turnbull three weeks before. Mathers, for one, had no trouble with morale. Mick Maguire, No. 9 Squadron armaments officer, could vouch for that:

'He came in to see me in the office and said; "Any chance of getting my aircraft out of the hangar?" I didn't know. I knew it had scaffolding all over it and was having all four engines changed. In any case, it would have to be air tested before it went on an op. He was back a few minutes later. "Will you put the bombs on in the hangar?" It was an HE bomb load that night. I wouldn't have been happy putting incendiaries on in a hangar. So he took the aircraft on ops without an air test. No time. They had faith, those pilots. Must have had.'

On New Year's Day, Mathers saw nothing of the target through the cloud, but did note 'a large column of black smoke rising to a height of about 27,000 feet', which was 6,500 feet above himself. Mathers went to Berlin again the next night, but not in EE136, which was back with Siddle for Stettin on 5 January. This town of 270,000 people on the river Oder, about 80 miles from Berlin, was a major shipbuilding centre and, with much commercial and industrial business, the capital city's port and gateway to the Baltic, so it is perhaps surprising that it had not warranted a large raid since 1941 when two attempts on this far-off target, by Wellingtons and Whitleys mostly, failed to cause serious damage.

On this occasion, Siddle thought the bombing was well concentrated, but a lot of it had drifted off target and much more could have resulted from 348 Lancasters and ten Halifaxes. Thirteen Lancasters and two Halifaxes were shot down and one more Lancaster ditched in the North Sea, out of petrol (all rescued).

Brunswick (Braunschweig) would probably not have attracted the bombers at this high point of the war, had it not become a provincial capital of Naziism and, consequently, a centre of arms manufacture. Before the war it had been noted for beer, sausages and all manner of minor industries. Then, it granted Adolf Hitler his German citizenship so he could stand for election as Chancellor, and thereafter became a kind of second Nürnberg. The first major raid was on 14 January. Siddle went in EE136 and, along with 495 other Lancasters, missed the place almost entirely. The night-fighters didn't miss and took most of the forty-one Lancasters lost that night, 8 per cent, for ten houses knocked down.

Of the forty-one, thirteen were Pathfinder Force, with five from No. 156 Squadron and three from No. 405 Squadron. Had Bill Siddle and his crew known this, maybe they wouldn't have transferred later in the month to No. 83 Squadron PFF. They would be all right; they all got through, as would B Flight Commander Flight Lieutenant Hadland's boys.

Three of his EE136 crew, Greenwood, Gaskell and Tirel, had been with Hadland at Bochum on 29 September 1943, when, coming home in darkness and cloud down to 500 feet, Hadland hadn't realised his altimeter wasn't working and put them in the drink off Mablethorpe. The engineer and the bomb aimer died; the rest bobbed about for nine hours in the dinghy before an air-sea rescue boat picked them up.

Now – 20 January 1944 – they were off to Berlin in WS/R with a VIP passenger, the station commander Group Captain 'Shorty' Pleasance, and Clayton Moore filling in at the back. Although liable to get in a lather when under pressure, 'Shorty' Pleasance was generally well regarded, a nice old boy, approachable, First World War veteran, no need to go on ops at all. He went to keep in touch with what his boys were facing routinely and it was this sense of duty that would bring about his death. While everyone else in EE136 that night would survive the war, Norman Pleasance went along for another ride to Frankfurt on 22 March with an experienced and well regarded crew (Flying Officer Manning and navigator Flying Officer James Hearn) and all were killed.

Hadland and his crew, apart from a regular rear gunner, transferred to No. 617 Squadron, Dambusters, on 15 February. With 617's reputation for suicidal special ops, such a posting might have been regarded with some suspicion, as if the dangers with No. 9 Squadron were insufficient, but 617 at this time was attacking precision targets in France, factories being employed in the German war effort – aero-engines, needle-bearings, Michelin tyres. Hadland and co went on seven of these ops and that was it. Tour expired. During his ten weeks there, No. 617 Squadron lost one Lancaster in action while No. 9 Squadron lost thirteen.

Flight Lieutenant Tex Turnbull – transferred to the USAAF – was on the last of his RAF tour, on 21 January; a trip to Magdeburg. All his operational reports from way back in July 1943 had been technical, about the flares, the marking, the accuracy of the bombing, and never a mention of fighters, flak hits, alarms and panics. If ever an exception could prove a rule, Turnbull was it. His reputation, stated in his DFC citation, also included 'high skill, fortitude and devotion to duty', but Magdeburg was a horrible night.

It was the first time the bombers had been in numbers to Magdeburg, the iron and steel town, a great trading place at the centre of the canal network, and they left it as they found it, or rather, didn't find it. Although the home comers thought they'd done a decent job, there was no actual recompense for twenty-three Lancasters down (plus one crashed at home out of petrol) and a horrifying thirty-seven Halifaxes, over 16 per cent of that type. Lancasters and Halifaxes both were mostly victims of night-fighters, and the bombing was awful.

Tex would have heard about another No. 9 Squadron American pilot, Anderson Storey, shot down the previous year and killed on his thirtieth operation, and maybe he thought about that when he was attacked by a fighter coming back. For fifteen minutes the two aircraft pirouetted about the sky, Lancaster gunners firing their .303 bullets for all their lives while German cannon and machine guns tore holes in the great bird. Both RAF and Luftwaffe crews claimed damage to the other, but not destruction, so William Wrigley Watts Turnbull could write to his mother to tell her he was fine, just fine.

Also fine were Australian Flight Sergeant Colin Peak and crew in EE136. They thought the bombing fair but scattered, and went in WS/R again on the next trip, Berlin, 27 January, and thought much the same. Peak was a young skipper, 21-years-old, nothing unusual about that, although his crewmen were older than most, average age twenty-five, and they had an American bomb aimer, Sergeant John Enoch Wilkes, known as Pappy, from Barrington, Rhode Island.

They'd had an extremely hairy first op to Berlin on 2 January 1944. They'd been first in line for take-off, not an easy thing for a sprog skipper with the rest of the squadron waiting behind. Also waiting were the fighters at the target, having had forty minutes' warning from their night watchmen. Pappy Wilkes, lying flat on his mat in his Perspex bomb-aimer's compartment, must have seen some of the twenty-seven Lancasters go down in flames, and then it was their turn. The gunners cried 'Corkscrew' and Peak threw the aircraft around. Now the gunners shouted that their guns had jammed, and an Me109 came in to help the Ju88 which was attacking them, and volunteer Pappy Wilkes may well have wished he'd stayed in the wooded, riverside, peaceful, small home town of Barrington.

Back at base concern increased; all were back bar two, a skipper with nineteen ops including five Berlins, Pilot Officer Glover, and the new boy, Peak. Nineteen was the life expectancy of a crew if you assumed 5 per cent losses per op, although the average at this time in the war was nearer thirteen. Glover was down at 0731 hours and went on to prove that averages are just that, mean points between high and low, and lived through the war. Peak, Wilkes and crew landed at 0734 hours after eight hours in the air, first up and last down, and lived to fight another night.

Their fourth op was in EE136 and, when they got back from Berlin on 27 January, Peak and crew would have learned that the one unlucky No. 9 Squadron Lancaster not returning that night had been with a skipper who was a quite remarkable young man among many remarkable men; Stanley James, a flight lieutenant with twenty ops behind him and yet still only nineteen years old when he died.

The Berlin war had to go on regardless, and on 28 January EE136 resumed what would become a long-lasting relationship with a lucky crew, Ron Mathers's. There was yet another Berlin on 30 January, attended by Mathers, James Ling and Harry Blow, but not EE136. Gunner Norman Wells was with Mathers as spare bod:

> 'We were going to Berlin. That was the heart of the war. But when we got there, God, it was horrendous. We all thought, we can't get through this. It was a mass of searchlights, and with the flak and the photoflashes going off and the bombs exploding, it was as bright as day. Nothing hit us, but we could see plenty of other aircraft going down, plenty.'

As on the night before, there was serious damage done to the city, but a lot of misses too. Out of almost 1,400 sorties on those three Berlin nights of 27/28/30 January, eighty-five Lancasters failed to return. Not too bad at 6 per cent, unless you considered that eighty-five Lancasters and crews was the equivalent of five entire squadrons disappearing in three nights. Add twenty-seven Halifaxes out of 323 sorties, over 8 per cent, and the battle of attrition at Berlin looked like it was going the way of the defenders.

Of course the Germans were suffering. Thousands were dead, hundreds of thousands were homeless, public transport was a mess, all sorts of industrial and public buildings were rubble – among the 'mountains' of wreckage (German report) were the ruins of the new Chancellery and the Ministry of Propaganda – but it was not the stuff of victory. After 30 January, all squadrons were stood down for a fortnight, with the exception of a little light mining, a few specialist ops and No. 617 Squadron's attack on a viaduct in southern France.

The stand-down was over on 15 February and the target was – Berlin. The stand-down had worked. Instead of sending a dozen or so aircraft as the best that could be managed under such pressure, No. 9 Squadron fielded twenty-one Lancasters and crews, easily the best show so far, in the largest force ever sent to Berlin, 891 Lancasters, Halifaxes and Mosquitos. This was really the grand finale of the battle; there was another raid to come in March, but the capital had not been destroyed and, with results like this, it never could be. Yes, there was extensive damage again, and with over 2,500 tons of bombs dropped, so there should have been, but it could never be a Hamburg.

And so to Leipzig on 19 February with EE136 on her fortieth, driven by Mathers. Everyone who came back from that op had to be a deeply affected man. The Germans took little notice of the diversion at Kiel and fighters got among the bombers from the Dutch coast onwards. As if that were not enough, winds were not as forecast and some squadrons got there early and had to mill about waiting for the pathfinders, to the delight of the home defences.

Mathers, Harry Blow, Bill Chambers with his Yankee bomb aimer, and Colin Peak with his, and the rest of No. 9 Squadron arrived as the pathfinders were dropping their TIs and Wanganui skymarkers and lost only one Lancaster out of the twenty that took off. Elsewhere in this large bomber force – 823 aircraft – it was much worse. There were seventy-nine Lancasters and Halifaxes shot down, the majority by fighters, and three more crashed without direct interference from the enemy. One in ten bombers – just about – were lost, for a cloud-covered target with scattered results.

The Luftwaffe saw this period of the air war as a victory. Leipzig was one of three key moments which, at the time, seemed to signal defeat and withdrawal for Bomber Command. The other two were to come: Berlin on 24 March and Nürnberg on 30 March, but, won as those fights were, the Luftwaffe would lose the campaign.

At Stuttgart, on 20 February, Mathers in EE136 had a spare bod in the mid-upper, Sergeant William Bingham, who would spend the rest of his short No. 9 Squadron career with the new B Flight commander, Squadron Leader Brian Montgomery Gilmour, DFC, a New Zealander on his second tour. That crew had nine ops before Munich on 24 April, when they were shot down by flak, all killed.

Future EE136 skipper, Pilot Officer Harry Forrest, was new – second Dicky Berlin, 15 February, first op Leipzig on 19 February, then Stuttgart. This was the night ex EE136 skipper Bill Chambers went down with all hands, two-thirds through his tour. Forrest would go on to complete a tour finishing in July. Contrast that with Pilot Officer Patrick Nice, whose first op had also been Leipzig. At Stuttgart he and crew were in a new Lancaster, LM447 WS/K, and no trace was ever found of machine or men. Or, consider Pilot Officer George Denson, who second Dickied on that Stuttgart night with a captain on his thirtieth, Paddy Ervine, who famously came into interrogation and said, 'I've corkscrewed all the way back from Stuttgart'. Denson went on his first op to Schweinfurt on 24 February, and there, he and his fellow novitiates were all killed.

Schweinfurt, population 50,000, was a market town too small to have had a Bomber Command raid so far but was a main centre of ball-bearing manufacture. This fitted C-in-C Harris's category of 'panacea' targets, of which he had a cynical view. These were picked by such as the Air Staff and the Ministry of Economic Warfare and forced on him against his better judgement and against his overall strategy. Their selection of Achilles tendons and jugular veins would, if severed, each do irreparable and catastrophic damage to the German war effort, said the men from the Ministry. These were always very difficult targets in one way or several, requiring disproportionate quantities of effort, risk and resources, which, Harris felt, should not be diverted from the main task.

Economics boffins might display great enthusiasm for, say, the molybdenum mine at Knaben, or the said ball-bearing factory at Schweinfurt, insisting that the consequences of their destruction would be invaluable for the war. Harris' men might well destroy such targets but the invaluable consequences never seemed to follow.

The Americans had been to Schweinfurt twice in 1943, doing considerable damage but with huge losses of men and machines approaching 30 per cent of forces sent. They were there again on the day before this raid, still losing aircraft and crews, but nothing like so many, but by now the Germans had dispersed much of their ball-bearing production away from Schweinfurt, so there wasn't so much left to hit and Bomber Command didn't hit it anyway.

March was a month of cancellations, eight of them, but there was plenty of blood and death otherwise. EE136 went to Stuttgart with Forrest, then to a new kind of target, a special attack on the aircraft factory at Marignane, on the outskirts of Marseille, by a small, select force on a return trip of nine and a half hours. Wing Commander Porter, No. 9 Squadron CO, led a force of forty-four Lancasters, including eleven from No. 9 Squadron, with Ron Mathers back in the driving seat of EE136. They had had some practice on time and distance runs bombing from what was, to Berlin habitués, low-level at around 8,000 feet. In bright moonlight, Porter dropped a red spot fire from 6,000 feet and got it 30 yards from the aiming point.

ORB: 'The target was well marked by the leading crew, as a result of which a most successful concentrated attack was made. Bombs were seen to fall amongst factory buildings and many fires were left burning. Little or no opposition was encountered.' Nor was the enemy seen coming home, flying at 200 feet most of the way.

That was the last piece of cake for quite a while; Mathers and EE136 were off to Stuttgart yet again, Frankfurt and Berlin. Stuttgart was a poor show with marking well out, but Frankfurt demonstrated what the bombers could do when well directed. With the RAF raid four nights before and the USAAF attack two days later, the city was devastated. German report:

'...their combined effect was to deal the worst and most fateful blow of the war to Frankfurt, a blow which simply ended the existence of the Frankfurt that had been built up since the Middle Ages.'

Berlin, 24 March, was more a demonstration of what the weather and the flak could do. EE136 went with Mathers who observed scattered fires. Harry Blow said the same thing. Harry Forrest said the fires were scattered over a wide area. Strong winds blew the bombers off track and the stream became as scattered as the bombing. With many individual targets to aim at, the radar-directed flak gunners scored heavily as the Lancasters and Halifaxes tried to find their way home, and that was the last of the 'Big City' for the big bombers.

Chapter Six

A Change of Course

Berlin was very bad; matters were about to reach the nadir. EE136 was laid off for a refit, so she didn't go on the worst night of them all, Nürnberg, 30 March 1944, but some of her graduates did. During what should have been a stand-down for the moon, the route was set according to a favourable weather forecast, with cloud on the way to the target and clarity over it. The likelihood of cloud had been contradicted by a scouting Mosquito crew, but there was no cancellation. As the bombers headed for the Nazi shrine, the moon shone brightly in a starry sky.

It was another very big raid with 795 bombers attacking a city not as famous for its industrial might as its special place in Nazi hearts. The defences were expected to be light, but through a combination of erratic winds and human errors the force became fragmented and the fighters were waiting.

Night-fighters by this time had the much improved air-to-air radar, the Lichtenstein SN2. It still had the drag-making array of antennae on the aircraft's nose, looking like four 1950s H-shaped TV aerials, but the reduction in speed mattered little compared with its ability to see through Window. In the moonlight, the German crews had, as it were, double vision.

Listening to their controller's commentary, the fighter pilots heard: 'Couriers flying in on a broad front between the mouth of the Scheldt and Ostend. Many hundreds. Course ninety degrees. Height 16,000 to 22,000 feet.'

The German expectation was that the bomber stream would soon turn, and perhaps turn again, before revealing the target for tonight. Instead, they churned on eastwards in a straight line. The fighter controllers were mystified, but they hadn't had the benefit of the British weather forecast.

Heading towards his assembly point above a radio beacon, Major Martin Drewes of III/NJG 1, in an Me110 fitted with Schrägermusik, ordered his radar operator Handke to turn on the Lichtenstein. The SN2 had two small, circular screens; one indicated direction of target, the other height. Handke was delighted to find three distinct signals on each.

'We are in the middle of the bomber stream,' he told his captain, who requested guidance to the nearest Tommy. Handke knew his business and, purely on his radar signals, took them within 1,000 yards.

'Ahead of us, and slightly higher,' said Handke.

This early version of the SN2 had a limitation; it didn't work any closer than 500 yards. Just as Handke called out 'six hundred yards', Drewes spotted the bomber, sparks coming from the four exhausts of a giant black cross silhouetted against the moonlit sky.

As they crept up on their prey, into the blind spot beneath its belly, they could see it was a Lancaster rather than a Halifax, and they could see the little underbelly dome that was the H2S air-to-ground radar fitted mainly to pathfinder aircraft. They might have wondered why there was no fighter detector there, or even a gun turret (as per original design) when Schrägemusik gave them such an advantage.

Through his reflector sight, Drewes aimed for the port inner engine; he knew that it ran the pump that powered the hydraulics for the gun turrets. Also, with the bomber on its outward journey, he didn't want a direct hit on the full bomb bay while flying as close as this.

He fired and soon the whole port wing was ablaze, which was the end of PFF No. 97 Squadron's ND390 OF/S, with second-tour men aboard including – pilot: Flight Lieutenant Desmond Rowlands, DFC – navigator: Flight Lieutenant Arthur Cadman, DFM – and tail gunner: Flight Lieutenant Richard Trevor-Roper, DFC, DFM, Gibson's gunner on the Dambusters raid.

Ten minutes later, Handke had another Tommy on his screens, high up at 23,000 feet. After a long climb, steered by the new miracle that was Lichtenstein SN2, Drewes found his quarry and settled in beneath it.

For the bomber crew, this had been, and was, a nerve-wracking time. They were still a hundred miles from the target and had already seen many flaming torches of falling aircraft. They had seen tracer in the sky, battles and explosions. Where was the cloud they'd been promised?

Drewes aimed his Schrägemusik, fired, and got off a few rounds before the guns jammed. The Lancaster pilot instantly put his machine into a sharp bank, then a steep dive, and minutes passed as he corkscrewed away from his invisible opponent. They'd thrown the fighter off. They must have thrown him off. No more shots, no sightings. Indeed, Drewes had had extreme difficulty in keeping up with the aerobatics and several times he thought he'd lost his Tommy, but there she was again, settled into normal flight and clearly visible.

Drewes dropped back a little, and down a little. He had no music to play so he lined up his Tommy in the old-fashioned way, pulled up into a steep climb and raked the Lancaster with his two nose-mounted cannon. Hundreds of 20mm shells hammered into the great bird's body. Immediately the Lancaster was on fire and diving. One parachute came out. Seconds later there was an explosion. Bits of the burning aircraft fell into the woods of the Vogelsberg; most of it and six dead bodies hit the ground near Butzbach.

Parachutist navigator, Sergeant Laws, was the only survivor. The rest – Flying Officer James Gordon Richmond Ling and all his crew from November and December when they'd flown together in EE136 WS/R, were killed.

The night-fighter attacks, which had begun as the bomber stream reached the Belgian border continued for an hour and Drewes added another to his score.

Those that got to the target did virtually no damage. Something like 100 ended up bombing Schweinfurt by mistake. The confusion was perhaps due to 'considerable fighter activity along the route south of the Ruhr and to consequent defensive manoeuvres' (No. 9 Squadron pilot's report, ORB). 'Another attack was seen in progress in the distance and it was thought that the correct target had not been identified' (No. 9 Squadron pilot's report, ORB).

Frank Belben was a flight engineer on the squadron since October 1943, so he'd seen a thing or two:

'That was a very stressful flight in, and even worse over what we thought was the target. From what we saw, we knew it was a night of heavy losses. We had a couple of fighter attacks but our gunners drove them off and we never got hit.'

Crews reported seeing so many going down in flames that they could only suppose it would be them next, a supposition reinforced by the number of fighter attacks being added to their personal experience. One of many was suffered by EE136 ex-skipper Harry Forrest.

SECRET: No. 9 Squadron Combat Report
Date: 30 March 1944: Pos: 50.30°N-08.40°E: Time: 0037hrs: Height: 20,000ft: Speed: 155 RAS: Course: 082°T: Target: Nürnberg: Lancaster 'V': Captain P/O Forrest
The Rear Gunner sighted a Ju88 at 250 yards starboard quarter down and gave the order corkscrew starboard. The E/A developed the attack from the position where it was first seen but did not open fire. The Rear Gunner fired about 500 rounds. The E/A was not seen to break away.

Soon after our A/C had resumed course it was attacked and damaged by an A/C which only the pilot saw as it broke away to port low down. He identified it as a Ju88 and clearly saw the green camouflage and black cross on its wing. During this attack the M/U Gunner was hit and died of his wounds during the trip. Neither of the Gunners fired during this attack as they did not see the E/A.

Wireless op was taking broadcast winds during the attack. Bomb doors were opened and aircraft dived, whereupon fire subsided. Continued on track over target and returned in concentration.

Weather: 3/10 cloud. ½ moon approx. Good vis. Searchlights: not exposed on the A/C.

Damage to own A/C: Two holes about 2ft square, one just forward of the Elsan, the other just aft of the MU turret. Pipe lines in the rear turret severed and a fire occurred. This was put out when the A/C went into a dive after the second attack. The leading edge of the starboard tailplane was hit and the starboard side of the fuselage aft of the MU turret was holed several times.

Damage to E/A: none claimed.

MU Gunner: F/Sgt Utting did not fire.

R Gunner: Sgt Pinchin 500 rounds.

Surviving Nürnberg, No. 9 Squadron crews also included those of Harry Blow, Ron Mathers, and Colin Peak with his American bomb aimer Pappy Wilkes, now 2nd Lieutenant USAAF, who thought he'd hit the target; in which case he was one of very few. Most bombs did nothing more than plough fields and uproot trees.

Over eighty bombers went down on the way to and at the target, and more on the way home. Including crashes due to errors and failures not enemy induced, Bomber Command lost 105 Halifaxes and Lancasters that night, over 13 per cent. First Lieutenant Helmut Schulte got four, Lt Doktor Wilhelm Seuss also, and 1st Lt Martin Becker shot down six Halifaxes on their way in, landed, refuelled, and felled another on its way home.

The Luftwaffe War Diaries claim that their Nürnberg success forced the RAF to admit defeat:

'It was the biggest night air battle of World War II and the total loss of 12 per cent of the operating force was too high even for British Command. The night air offensive was suspended, its failure being plain. But if the German night-fighters had won their greatest victory of the war, it was also their last.'

There was certainly more than a grain of truth in this, but a consideration at least equal to night-fighter success was the need to prepare the ground for the coming invasion of France by the Allies. No. 9 Squadron had already been to two French railway targets before Nürnberg, and that was now to be the way of it with the occasional German interruption.

There were three key elements of strategy necessary for the perfect invasion of the French coast. The enemy had to be prevented from being able to reinforce his armies; the landing place had to be rendered defenceless before the landing; and the enemy must not be strong enough to prevent the invaders from breaking out and advancing into open country. Perfection could not be achieved but Bomber Command was expected to create circumstances as near to it as possible. The first task was the complete paralysis of the railway system from the Rhine to the French coast and a list was drawn up of seventy-nine targets in France, Belgium and Germany. The US 8th Air Force took on a large slice, the Allied Expeditionary Air Force took some, the US 15th Air Force took a few, and Bomber Command took the most. Marking was usually by high-flying Oboe Mosquitos, although sometimes it was done visually at low-level.

Germany was not entirely left alone and crews could find themselves flying on moonless nights to German targets and on moonlit nights to French ones: railways, armaments factories, garrisons, the logistics and resources which would be important to German countermeasures against the invaders. In the previous year, 1943, Bomber Command had dropped 175 per cent of the tons of bombs dropped altogether in 1939, '40, '41 and '42; the bombers were doing six times the business their predecessors had. Now the rate was upped again, and 1944 would see twice as many heavy bombers as in 1943, doing three times the work. Nevertheless, it was thought at HQ that raids over France would be much less dangerous for aircrew than flying over Germany.

This would never do. Why, after originally defining a tour as 200 operational flying hours, then as thirty operations, almost all of them over Germany, it seemed to some of the brass hats that northern occupied France was offering a new kind of tour, of thirty nearby picnics. The prospect of waste, of seeing a Germany-hardened crew transfer to safety, tour expired, filling in the last of their logbooks with a quick half-dozen Sunday School outings, was too awful and so a French op would henceforth count only as one third of a German one.

Such a raid was on the railway yards at Tours, 180 Lancasters on the night of 10 April. Pappy Wilkes hadn't flown since Nürnberg. In the meantime he'd been granted a new rank, Flight Officer, invented by the USAAF to correspond more closely with the RAF's Pilot Officer. Only one Lancaster went down on this raid and that was DV198 WS/U-Uncle, veteran of fifty trips. The Australian skipper was Colin Peak; he and his crew had flown fifteen completed ops, and they'd been together all the time except for Marignane when another stood in for Wilkes. It was such a long time since they'd escaped with corkscrews and jammed guns from attacks by a Ju88 and an Me109, second day of the new year over Berlin on their first trip. The flak found the Uncle over the target and she fell into a Tours suburb called St-Pierre-des-Corps, with seven bodies.

Harry Blow finished his tour, Ron Mathers became flight lieutenant and flight commander, and the squadron carried on with their thirds until 3 May, when a disaster with several causes forced a rethink, attacking the German army base at Mailly-le-Camp, the depot of the 21 Panzer Division and a big centre for tank training. Confusion over the marking and failures in radio comms had the bombers hanging around far too long, and forty-two out of 346 Lancasters were shot down, mostly by fighter crews who could cut and come again among their circling foes. French ops henceforth counted as one.

EE136's next was one of those designed to keep the Germans in Germany; to Duisberg on 21 May, with a crew including three Canadians and headed by her most frequent driver-to-be, Pilot Officer Roy 'Puddle' Lake. Their first had been to Toulouse at the start of the month, when only four Lancasters were lost out of 402.

The force for Duisburg was 500+, with nineteen from No. 9 Squadron – one crew on their last, four on their first and fourteen at various stages between. They would have known little about the place except it would be heavily defended. They didn't know that this would be the fourteenth time that Lancasters had been there, or that almost fifty of those Lancasters had been lost in the process. Nor, of course, had they any idea that another thirty would go down tonight.

Any of them paying attention to their old geography master might have been able to tell the others that Duisburg, population 430,000, sat where the Rhine met the Ruhr and was a huge industrial and railway centre. By way of the Rhine-Herne and Dortmund-Ems canals, its port – one of the biggest inland ports in Europe – connected with the North Sea. Never mind all that. How many ack-ack guns and night-fighters did it have?

There was cloud, but the marking was generally good and they did serious damage, although 'Puddle' Lake got slightly lost, saw no marking and bombed Mönchengladbach, 30 miles to the south-west.

They were away again the next night, to Brunswick, another cloud-covered failure exacerbated by the master bomber's u/s radio and, five days later, on EE136's fiftieth, to the railways and workshops at Nantes, had more technical trouble. 'Controller's messages were unintelligible.' 'No messages received by W/T or R/T.' Some of the crews saw the markers, some saw nothing, some bombed, some didn't. The ones that did wrecked the target and only one out of 100 Lancasters was lost, crashing at home, nobody injured.

Railways at Saumur and a German signals station at Ferme d'Urville, near Cherbourg, were similarly destroyed by small, specialised forces of 5 Group Lancasters featuring Lake and EE136, followed by a D-Day raid to Argentan on 6 June. This was another railway target but the emphasis was changing. As well as German transport and communications, targets in France now included troops, gun emplacements and E-boat bases, plus a major effort against the synthetic oil industry in the fatherland and shortly, repeated attempts to find and destroy the launch sites of the new revenge weapon, the V1 rocket, the doodlebug, that was never going to win the war for Hitler but would become a daily terror for London.

This was a very busy time for the bombers. Railways at Rennes and Poitiers were hit by Lake and the only other EE136 graduate still flying, Harry Forrest; Ron Mathers was done and off to an instructor post to await his DFC. Troops at Aunay-sur-Odon, near Caen, and fuel dumps at Châtellerault were successfully attacked with no losses, but then it was back to Germany.

The regularly visited and constantly repaired synthetic oil refineries near Gelsenkirchen were split into two targets for 21 June; 133

Lancasters and six Mosquitos went to Wesseling, 123 and nine went to Scholven-Buer.

This was in a different league from recent ops. Every trip was dangerous from all kinds of angles, but hot targets in the Ruhr, Happy Valley, had everything, including large numbers of night-fighters. Flak would be intense. There would be no peace as the bomber stream went in. All around them would be the silent but constant red flashes of anti-aircraft shells exploding, fired from guns which had a neat white circle painted on their barrels for every Tommy shot down.

The entire available strength of No. 9 Squadron took off, nineteen of them, between 2300 and 2330 hours, for Scholven-Buer; the newer boys on the squadron were in for a shock. In bombing practice over southern England, on the Salisbury ranges, they'd bombed red and green target indicators from 7,000 feet and these were the sort of heights they'd bombed at in France, so they could be super-accurate and avoid hitting their French allies. Over Germany, they were way up there at 20,000 feet, as far away as possible from the flak; and never mind about allies, there weren't any.

At the other target, Wesseling, No. 44 Squadron lost six, No. 57 Squadron lost five and No. 619 Squadron lost five. Altogether, thirty-eight Lancasters went down on the Wesseling raid, almost one out of every three, in compensation for little damage done. For similarly little result at Scholven-Buer, seven Lancasters were shot down by night-fighters on route, plus another that struggled home to crash, plus one to the flak – 7 per cent.

Pilot Officer Leslie Wood arrived on squadron on 31 May, second Dickied with Harry Forrest to Cherbourg, and now continued his France-only experience in EE136 to the railways at Limoges. Nobody was lost on that one and the target was wrecked, but it was a different story the next night, moonlit, looking for V-bomb launching sites, on EE136's sixtieth. They were part of a massive exercise, 500 Lancasters and over 230 other bombers hitting seven different targets. Doodlebugs were becoming a real menace, knocking out railway stations, telephone exchanges, factories and hospitals, cutting power supplies and, of course, killing people; well over 1,000 by this time.

The aiming point for No. 9 Squadron was Prouville, where they could expect intense opposition from the night-fighters that packed the Somme/Pas de Calais region, but their first crew to go down hardly had time for fighting. Way back in February, Pilot Officer Ronald 'Ginger' Craig had been on his second Dicky with EE136 skipper James Ling, killed in March at Nürnberg. Craig had himself recently taken future EE136 pilot Ron Adams to Scholven-Buer.

The searchlights found him just over the French coast at only 12,000 feet. The flak hit time and time again; bombs were jettisoned but it was too late. Ginger Craig was an old lag, tour of thirty ops nearly done, and he was still only twenty years of age when he died.

Canadian Pilot Officer Harold Rae and his crew had had a much shorter career; a fortnight to be exact. Harry Forrest had taken him second Dicky to Rennes; then it had been Aunay, Poitiers, Scholven-Buer, Limoges, bang, they exploded in the skies over the Pas de Calais. The mid-upper somehow got out of the aircraft but nobody else did.

Flight Sergeant John Halshaw, twelve ops, had with him on this night an extra man and an experiment, a belly gun that harked back to the original design but never caught on. The gunner was Sergeant W. Wilson, who had flown with Ron Mathers in EE136, and he and the rear gunner survived the night-fighter attack and the crash while the others did not.

It would be a while before Pilot Officer Adams took the controls of EE136; meanwhile, he was a new pilot taking his crew on their second op. They'd been to Limoges the night before. For Prouville, his ORB report stated: 'The aircraft was damaged'. In more detail, he might have described his port outer engine on fire, one rudder and fin shot away, six feet of port wing ditto and cannon-shell holes the length of the fuselage.

The damage occurred during the 'second of three combats within five minutes of the target area, after several dummy runs had been made. Coned continuously from the time of crossing the enemy coast. Bomb load jettisoned during combat in target area.'

The searchlight technique here was to try and hold the bomber long enough for a night-fighter to fly down the beam, where the pilot would think himself more or less invulnerable because the gunners would be dazzled. Sergeant Fred Whitfield was Ron Adams's rear gunner:

'Prouville was considered to be an easy trip, as it was just a few miles inside the French mainland. The run to the target was straightforward and when we arrived over the target we had to orbit to allow the Pathfinders to drop their TIs. At that moment we were caught by 30–40 searchlights. I spotted an Me109 coming straight up the searchlight beam from starboard toward our aircraft. I gave the skipper immediate instructions to corkscrew starboard. The skipper reacted without delay. I fired my four Brownings at the attacking fighter and watched four lines of tracer bullets striking the fighter's fuselage which broke away in flames.

'There was hardly time to think when a second fighter joined in the attack. This one was a twin engined Ju88 which attempted to follow us through the corkscrew manoeuvre. I fired but didn't seem to be making any impression as the bullets seemed to be bouncing off. He kept on coming and fired a long burst at me which appeared like a sheet of flame. My next sensation was a blast of cold air and I felt as if I was sitting outside the turret. My turret had been hit, but I was untouched and I continued to fire at the oncoming fighter. Flames then began surging from one of his engines and he rolled onto his back and passed below us.

'Almost immediately another Me109 came at us and Frank Stebbings in the mid- upper turret spotted him and I watched his tracer bullets flying over my head as he caught the fighter. I fired my four guns immediately as he rolled onto his back and passed beneath us. Then things went quiet. However, we hadn't got away with it unscathed. The Ju88 had hit our port outer engine and set it on fire. We pressed on and went into the bombing run and bombed the target. We hadn't flown very far (homewards) when the skipper said the controls felt heavy.'

Skipper's report: 'Off track on return after combat, believed crossed English coast off Dungeness, skirting London to west of Reading'.

Whitfield: 'When we landed we were amazed at the amount of damage our Lanc had sustained. How it remained airborne seemed to be a miracle,* but it really was due to our skipper's skilful flying. I will never forget his face when he removed his oxygen mask; he was quite drawn and pale. After that op, our skipper got the nickname "Lucky".'

Leslie Wood, more experienced than the drawn and pale but lucky Adams – he'd been on six ops – also jettisoned his bombs while he was coned by searchlights and shot at by flak, immediately after he'd escaped from 'an encounter with an enemy aircraft', as he phrased it, but did not earn a nickname.

He was in charge of EE136 again, next time out, to more railways at Vitry-le-François on the River Marne, where skippers grumbled about the controller's orders changing so often, but these were difficult targets, long and thin, so awkwardly shaped for bombing, and French casualties had to be as few as humanly possible.

---

* It never flew again.

The brief for the month of July was more transport targets to help the invasion, and V-bomb sites, code named No Ball, part of the long-standing Operation Crossbow against the world's first ballistic missiles. These *Vergeltungswaffen* – revenge weapons – would include Werner von Braun's V2 space rocket prototype, but for now there was just the V1 flying bomb, the autopiloted, aimed, rather than guided, missile. Hitler came to northern France to see for himself and was immensely proud of the German nation which was able to fight with weapons so advanced. He assigned top priority to production of 3,000 doodlebugs a month. The feeling among V1 field commanders was that 100 a day was nowhere near enough to force a victory in the war, which the ultimate objective of the V-weapon programme. After all, Bomber Command had flattened half of urban Germany and that hadn't won the war.

By 15 June, the Germans had set up fifty-five launching sites in France. By noon the next day almost 250 doodlebugs had been fired, destroying nine of their own launching sites and a French village and mostly missing London, but by midnight London had taken seventy-three hits and one bug had doodled all the way into deepest Suffolk before dropping harmlessly into a field. By July, manufactured at a furious pace by Volkswagen at a unit cost of £125 (about £5,000 modern), they were an everyday, well organised terror. There was no effective defence against them, and the citizens of London could see and hear this weird new kind of weapon, with an effect on spirits not unlike those earlier times when silent, unassailable Zeppelin airships had dropped another weird new weapon, bombs, on London in the First World War.

First up of the No Balls was Creil – target as listed in the ORB – a small town 65 miles from the coast in Oise, but, more specifically, the nearby village of Saint-Leu-d'Esserant, where there was a network of caves and natural tunnels which the locals had been using for growing mushrooms. The Germans threw out the mushrooms and the villagers and, seeing a series of bomb-proof shelters ready-made, stored in the caves large quantities of V-weapons and associated supplies, more, probably, than at any other site. Here the Germans were assembling doodlebugs and taking them by road to the launching points. Bombing was not going to wreck the caves altogether, but it could bring a lot of rock down to block the entrances and it could make a mess of the immediate area, smashing up the roads and railways and making normal use very difficult.

Earlier in the day, 4 July, the same target had been attacked by the Lancasters of No. 617 Squadron, carrying Barnes Wallis's super-bomb, the 12,000lb Tallboy. Now it was a clear, moonlit night with the promise of plenty of fighters about. Railway raids on Orleans and Villeneuve helped spread the fighters more thinly, but there were many battles going and coming back, thirteen of them fatal to bombers (one from No. 9 Squadron).

Leslie Wood was there, and Charles Scott, who would be in EE136 next time, and in our machine tonight were George Langford and crew. Langford had had his second Dicky in early May so those boys were well on their way, half a tour completed – Creil was their sixteenth op together – and it was a good attack, well concentrated, with one No. 9 Squadron Lancaster failing to return out of fourteen.

The decommissioning of the caves at Saint-Leu-d'Esserant had to be put beyond doubt; doodlebugs were now droning in at more than Hitler's hundred a day. Deaths in London had reached 2,500. If the first raid had softened up the target, another should flatten it so No. 9 Squadron was ordered back immediately and only low cloud stopped them going until 7 July. Taking part then were 208 Lancasters, with fourteen from Bardney.

Again, the bombers had fine moonlight to work in, and there were many other eyes glad of the silver disc that illuminated the bombers' targets and against which a Lancaster silhouetted beautifully. Everybody in No. 9 Squadron who got home had been shot at. They were all damaged, every one. Of the force of 208 Lancasters, thirty-one did not get home, most of those victories for night-fighters, plus one badly damaged and crashing at home, makes losses of 15 per cent.

No. 106 Squadron lost five, No. 207 Squadron likewise, and several squadrons lost three, including No, 9 Squadron, among whom were George Langford and his ever-present crew; four killed, including an unusual rear gunner, Geoffrey Baseden, a 38-year-old chartered accountant.

Against these awful losses and those of the previous attack, the caves of Saint-Leu, whimsically anglicised in the squadron ORB as St Len, had been blocked, rendered u/s, with goodness knows how many souls buried alive. Wehrmacht Colonel Walter of the special purpose V-weapon army unit, the 65th Corps, was there:

> 'You could hear a constant rumbling overhead, and began to feel that the very mountain was on the move and might collapse at any moment. It was asking too much of any man's nerves to expect him to hold out in caves like that.'

Through this and other No Ball attacks in the middle fortnight of July, the rate of doodlebugs hitting London was cut in half.

At Bardney, on 10 and 11 July, ops were cancelled, but not the practice. On the night of the 12 July, twelve went to Culmont-Chalindrey, a railway target in the Haute-Marne. EE136 was back in the charge of 'Puddle' Lake, who also took her to more railways at Nevers, central France, south of Paris, then long-serving (and lucky) Flying Officer Sheppard took her to German army targets at Caen, a dawn raid on 18 July, up at around 0400 hours, down at about 0730 hours. Allied armies were struggling to break through strong enemy positions and the bombers, around 1,000 including 667 Lancasters, the most to fly so far, were sent in to pave the way by hitting half a dozen fortified villages around the town with 5,000 tons of bombs. Large numbers of tanks and other vehicles were destroyed and those that were left could hardly move for bomb craters. Many, many German soldiers were killed and wounded and the invading Allies found hundreds wandering about, dazed with shock and unable to resist capture.

Only one Lancaster had been lost in the Caen dawn, when no fighters turned up, but it was a different story that night. The targets were railways and 5 Group sent around 250 Lancasters split into two forces. The larger, just short of 150, went to Aulnoye-Aymeries, a town on the Oise near the Belgian border, where they had a relatively bloodless time of it. The smaller force went to the railway junction at Revigny-sur-Ornain on the Champagne/Lorraine border. At 2300 hours on the 18 July, No. 9 Squadron took off for Revigny, making two ops in one day for some crews. Two previous attacks on Revigny had resulted in no fatal damage done except to seventeen Lancasters out of 232. This night, 109 were going.

The German fighters were in the air, ready, as the bombers crossed the coast. Lucky Adams corkscrewed his way to the target and corkscrewed his way back under more or less constant attack while he and his crew saw what seemed like dozens of aircraft falling in flames. It was testimony to the ability of a Lancaster to take punishment that they got home.

Leslie Wood, one of the May intake; pilot of EE136 twice in June, took off at 2301 hours for Revigny. On that terrible night, a great many tours of operations were ended prematurely. Proportionately, enemy fighters had one of their best bags ever and almost a quarter of the force went down. Adams and his men were right. They had seen dozens; two dozen, in fact. No. 619 Squadron alone lost five, No. 49 Squadron four, No. 630 Squadron likewise, and No. 9 Squadron lost

Leslie Wood and crew, with only the navigator, Flight Sergeant Oates, taken prisoner. The rest were taken to the graveyard, as were so many more who were lost in the cause of Revigny junction. At least they'd cut the railway this time.

Of the fifteen pilots and crews arriving at No. 9 Squadron in the month of May, eight had been lost by mid-July and the other seven were roughly halfway through their tours. 'Puddle' Lake and crew in EE136 were a little further on than that and they, like everyone else, came back from a V-bomb site near the small village of Thierny (Presles-et-Thierny), and flew again next day to Courtrai or Kortrijk, over the border into Belgium, another key railway target linking Germany and occupied Holland with northern France. The official report of the Courtrai raid, 20/21 July, said that the rail junctions and yards were devastated, which, of course, was what 300 Lancasters could do to a railway. It was a straightforward trip for most. Adams even did two camera runs over the target to make sure he got the evidence that it was thoroughly pasted.

EE136 missed another devastating op to Kiel but was back in business for Donges, Atlantic coast, today a major oil-tanker terminal and refinery by the mouth of the Loire, then an asset to the Germans. The captain of EE136 was Flight Lieutenant Edward Relton, unusual for his age, being thirty-four, and for being one of three pioneers of a new practice, sending pilots out without a second Dicky flight. The ancient and much hallowed routine had been stopped, because of the losses of so many trained novitiates who never had a chance of doing the job for real.

Not an Australian himself, being from West Kirby in the Wirral, Relton had collected an all-Aussie crew apart from the flight engineer. They had been to Caen on their first, Revigny, Courtrai, where a fellow no-second-Dicky went down with his crew on their third op (Flying Officer Graham Garlick aged twenty), and Kiel.

Givors was yet another French railway target, in the south this time, on the Rhône just below Lyon. The raid, on 26 July, was not a triumph for No. 9 Squadron. 'Puddle' Lake came home early in EE136 with the rear turret u/s, Harry Forrest jettisoned, and Adams was late getting away and couldn't catch up. Sixteen set off; Scott, Sheppard and six more got there and bombed. The reason was the weather. Bob Woolf was an Australian wireless operator who remembered the flight well:

'Givors was an eight and three quarter hour trip in extremely poor weather. We were in electrical storms continually and the whole aircraft was alive with St Elmo's Fire. There were static sparks everywhere and the exterior was covered with blue flames. Aerials, guns and wings were brilliantly alight. The props were just four circles of flame. Visibility was almost zero, though enough for us to see three aircraft hit by flak and go down very close to us. There were hailstones. Rain poured into the aircraft making the floor awash with water. In such foul weather there would be no fighters about so the Master Bomber gave the order to turn on navigation lights. Immediately the surrounding sky was filled with red, green and white lights showing just how close and heavily populated the bomber stream was. It was terrifying. Surprisingly, we later learned that the attack had been quite successful. Not surprisingly, the hailstones had stripped the paint off our aircraft.'

There was one pilot and crew who didn't care any more about the weather. Flying Officer Harry Forrest – who had had his mid-upper killed over Nürnberg back in March – had done it. Tour complete. He could have a few weeks' leave now, a posting to a conversion unit and a DFC in November when they got around to it.

Stuttgart was a difficult target and Bomber Command had been unable to make much of an impression on it so far. Although a fair size – half a million people – the city was spread over hills and valleys and the central areas had proved hard to hit. Famous for wine and publishing, but also for Daimler-Benz building aircraft engines, tanks and trucks, Bosch making all kinds of electrical gear, and as a railways hub, Stuttgart needed to be demolished. A series of three raids in five nights at the end of July went a long way towards that aim. Lake was there in EE136, so were Adams, Sheppard and Scott, and no-one from the squadron was lost, although many others, on this moonlit night were – forty Lancasters out of 494, 8 per cent – mostly to night-fighters and mostly on the way there.

Never a dull moment in Bomber Command, the crews may have thought at their next briefing: a daylight to the Normandy battle area, in front of an American advance. The Yanks were probably not greatly impressed when, on a cloudy morning, half the force of 700 didn't drop any bombs at all, including Charles Scott in EE136 and the rest of No. 9 Squadron, and only two of the six aiming points received useful punishment.

More railways next evening, bombing in Burgundy around 2230 hours at Joigny-La-Roche, a daylight, which at least meant fighter escorts and no resistance apart from the flak. EE136 was being driven by a pilot with a high reputation as a technical flier, Flying Officer Doug Tweddle. The WAAF battle-order typists took a while to stop calling him Tweedle; another WAAF, Nancy Bower, who worked in the officers mess bar, remembered him:

'Tweddle was married and his wife used to ring up, which was a difficulty most of them didn't have. We weren't allowed of course to say where he was, but we'd say, "He's just not around at the moment" and she knew by that he was flying.'

Flying to Joigny and back presented no problems – 'Aiming point clearly identified visually. Target area seemed to be plastered with bombs' – but next day the squadron couldn't find their V-bomb site in the clouds so were ordered home. This, the Mont Candon site north of Rouen, was one of the permanent set-ups with block buildings, storage, flak batteries and so on, but from the air it was no more than a farm in the woods.

That was Lake's nineteenth trip in EE136, and they went again the following afternoon, 1 August, to a V-bomb store, Bois de Cassan in the Forêt de L'Isle-Adam, Val-d'Oise, only twenty miles or so from Paris. Pilots of No. 9 Squadron thought the bombing scattered and the leadership poor, but the official report claims success. 'Puddle' Lake's score of trips in EE136 WS/R had been with the same crew throughout, apart from two single substitutions, and the aircraft now had seventy-five little bombs and ice-cream cones (for Italian ops) on her nose.

Chapter Seven

76 to 93 in 11 Weeks

The village of Trossy, by the small town of Saint-Maximin, in the same limestone-quarrying district as Saint-Leu, had V1 rockets being put together and stored in its natural shelters. There was a big raid on 3 August, one of quite a long run of daylights for No. 9 Squadron. The flak was intense but that was part and parcel; what aircrew remembered was the traffic congestion. One said:

'The briefing officers told us to look out for a vic of Lancs with white stripes on their tail planes, and to throttle back to let them get to the front. Some crews saw them and some didn't, so some throttled back and some didn't, which meant we weren't so evenly spread out. Then the leaders went off track, then came back on, which bunched us up even more.'

Some skippers, perhaps inexperienced, tried too hard to avoid the flak and, in the crowded sky, crashed into other bombers. Fred Whitfield was in EE136 with Lucky Adams:

'We saw two planes crash together alongside us, and the last I saw was pieces of aircraft floating down to earth. We stuck our noses down and got below the rest of them for safety. While the anti-aircraft fire was bursting about four thousand feet above us we were quite safe and got home.'

The general view was expressed by Australian wireless operator Bob Woolf:

'We took off at 11.45 on a beautiful day with pretty cloud formations and bombed rocket installations near Paris from 17,500 feet. Flak was very accurate but not too thick. We saw one kite go down, hit by falling bombs (LM163 CF/J of No. 625 Squadron; two men killed, the rest POW). This packing in close on the run-up to bomb is deadly. They should stagger the formations more. Two hundred Lancs weaving in and out can be a nuisance. It's bad enough without all that.'

While EE136 had a week off, Flying Officer Sheppard finished his tour and 'Puddle' Lake had a close shave bombing a bridge at Étaples. ORB: 'Target not attacked as when on bombing run a steep turn to port had to be made to avoid bombs dropped by another Lancaster from not more than 100 feet above. This Lancaster had previously crossed three times.' Lake knew who it was; not one of the aldermen like Scott, Adams, or Sheppard. One of the new boys had got over excited.

To that point, the squadron had operated on fifteen days out of seventeen. Ground crew and armourers had hardly seen their beds but nobody ever gave them a gong.

Back on duty to the Givors railways again on 11 August, EE136 had a new crew captained by Canadian Flight Lieutenant Camsell, taking part in an exceptionally accurate attack along with new skipper and soon to be EE136 man, the American, Flight Sergeant John Edward Stowell, known as Jesse, of Royal Oak, Detroit, Michigan, and Burnley, Lancashire. He'd been born in November 1921, in Royal Oak, but his English parents had returned to the UK in 1932 where the boy, then known as Ed, grew up into an engineering apprenticeship and thence into the air force as a mechanic. He wanted to be a pilot and, after a lot of hard work, got there.

Another new boy on the squadron was Sergeant Les Keeley. Sergeant pilots were a rarity by this stage but he and Stowell would be officers by the end of the month. WAAF Nancy Bower:

'Keeley was a very popular chap, and he was another of the cheeky ones. There were many different types; it was no indicator of whether they'd last or not. You could have the anything–goes sort like Keeley, or the top–drawer officers, but they got the same results.'

Brest, 13 August, and EE136 was back with Lake again. The objective was to sink a tanker which the Germans were going to use to block the harbour. Lake saw bombs hit the ship and others saw the same, but one captain (Ray Harris, on his twenty-fifth op, aged twenty) saw something else too, of an ex EE136 crew:

'It was Relton in O-Oboe, he was flying right alongside. Some of them said he was hit by flak. My own bomb aimer, Jim Parsons said it was flak, but I saw him at 16,000 feet being hit by bombs dropped by another Lanc flying above us. They could have hit me but they hit him, and there was no doubting the result. The nose was gone and half the starboard wing was missing. They tipped over and went straight in, into the shore by the harbour. Nobody could have survived.'

It was the only bomber lost on that trip and nobody survived. Flight Lieutenant Edward Harry Maxwell Relton, aged thirty-four, was on his twelfth op. His wife was staying in Bardney village. They had been married one week.

Next day, No. 9 Squadron was given another ship to destroy for the same reason, not a rusty hulk but a new one this time, the battleship *Clémenceau*, which had begun construction in 1939 ready for the war but had been overtaken by events. Lake was there on his penultimate of twenty-three in EE136 and, in very heavy flak, thought everybody missed it.

The German army was trapped on the Brest peninsula but still fighting hard to prevent the Allies from taking the harbour, which would then be able to accept shipping direct from the USA and greatly increase supplies to the invasion forces. General Patton had issued his famous order, 'Take Brest', on 1 August. Brest, like the other U-boat bases, had been classified as *Festung* (fortress, to be held at all costs) and, despite the expectations set up by these air raids, the Americans wouldn't get in until 18 September, by which time they had lost 10,000 men and the docks had been smashed to pieces by bombs and artillery so they were not much use anyway – and the front line by then was 500 miles away.

The eightieth op for EE136 was to a night-fighter base in The Netherlands, Gilze Rijen, part of a massive effort against nine military airfields, and part of the preparations for a new bomber offensive against Germany, which, unlike most of the work lately, would be back into the darkness. The squadron all bombed within one and a half minutes. The base was obliterated. The runways were hit and the whole airfield was plastered with bombs. The woods around the airfield were set on fire. Ed Stowell was flying EE136, and Gilze Rijen was the first op for another American skipper-to-be of our heroine machine, but not so lucky, a quiet man also from Michigan, Clifford Newton.

Newton took EE136 to the U-boat pens at La Pallice on the west coast of France on 16 August, a joint operation with No. 617 Squadron, whose Tallboy bombs had penetrated the massively thick concrete roofs on previous raids. Although the damage had been considerable, the real disaster for the Germans lay in the shattering of their belief in the pens as impregnable, bomb proof, free from the worry of aerial attack. They didn't have to worry much on this occasion; so thick was the cloud cover that only Newton and two others saw the target and bombed.

Two days later, Flight Sergeant Bradford took his crew on their first op, La Pallice again, in EE136, flew one more (Ijmuiden), was promoted to pilot officer and posted to Coastal Command at Eastchurch. His whole crew was taken over by Flying Officer Ernie Redfern, one of the May intake – second Dickie with Ron Mathers – who had finished his tour of thirty but, like several, including 'Puddle' Lake, had opted to stay on for another fifteen with the end of the war seemingly in sight.

Redfern and his original crew had achieved – where so many had failed – a tour of bomber ops, and they were all of four months older than when they started. That was one way of measuring their achievement; they had managed to stay alive for four months. Such achievements were rarely seen twice, which was why they didn't volunteer alongside their skipper, took their non-combat postings and left Ernie to find himself a new lot.

Fourteen of No. 9 Squadron, including EE136 – with another new crew led by Aussie Flying Officer A.F. Jones – attacked the E-boat pens at Ijmuiden with very good results on 24 August, and there was another ship in Brest harbour to sink three days later, with Flight Sergeant Keeley in charge of EE136.

That was the last op for No. 9 Squadron for a while, with practice instead on the first four days of September. There were experiments to see how fuel economy could be maximised, which combinations of propellor pitch and throttle settings would yield the most miles per gallon when fully loaded – and more than fully loaded. Clearly there was to be a very special mission indeed, a long way away. Nobody taking part in those experiments had the slightest idea about why they were doing it; the build-up to Operation Paravane had begun; the first *Tirpitz* raid.

The awe-inspiring battleship *Tirpitz*, sister ship to the *Bismarck*, was a weapon of mass destruction before that phrase was ever coined. She had eight fifteen-inch guns, twelve six-inch, sixteen four-inch, eight quad torpedo tubes and a huge number of anti-aircraft guns. She could steam at over 30 knots, had a range of 9,000 miles at 19 knots and was manned by 2,400 crew. Presumably because there were no plans for her to have to go through the Panama Canal, her designers had made her much wider in beam than her length (260 yards) would normally require, thus making her a very stable and accurate gun platform. She would alter the balance of power wherever she went.

Any direct attack on her in a conventional naval engagement would bring heavy losses to the attackers. The deadly calculation – would the losses be worthwhile if the *Tirpitz* was sunk? – could not be made with any certainty, partly because of her armour. From six and a half feet below the waterline to the gun battery deck above, she had armour plating over a foot thick. Above that it was six inches thick. Three and four-inch armour protected her vitals from the enemy in the sky; like the U-boat pens, she was designed to expect and to be able to resist all forms of aerial attack by any bomb or torpedo known about at that time.

Churchill ordered *Tirpitz* must be destroyed, and over the months – which turned into years – more than thirty attempts were made by over 700 British, Russian and American aircraft and midget submarines.

Sir Arthur 'Butch' Harris later told the short story of how the job of sinking the *Tirpitz* was passed to him. Harris's view was that such a mission could only be the result of a mating between a red herring and a wild goose:

'Churchill rang me and said, "I want you to sink the *Tirpitz*". I said, "Why bother, Prime Minister? She's not doing any harm

where she is." Churchill replied, "I want you to sink the *Tirpitz*".
So I sent the boys out and they sank the *Tirpitz*.'

The boys in question were those of Nos. 9 and 617 Squadrons, and
sending them out was not quite so simple as Harris implied. 'Where
she is', was beyond the Arctic Circle, in a fjord. The northern winter
was coming and with it the short days that would postpone the job
into next year, making it more likely that the Germans would commit
Tirpitz to battle as the Allies took charge of the war. If the boys were
to be sent, it would have to be soon, and September was a poor month
for bombing weather in those parts. They would go with the Tallboy
bomb, the weapon designed to cause earthquakes underneath buildings.
Regardless of what it had been designed for, there was little doubt that
Tallboy was the only bomb which could slice through *Tirpitz*'s armour
plate.

She was anchored in Kåfjord, way up there near the top of Norway
and too far for a there-and-back raid, even for Lancasters modified
well beyond specification. Overload tanks could be installed and, to
save weight, the mid-upper turret could be removed, likewise the
armour plating around the pilot. With a six-ton Tallboy bomb and full
tanks, the all-up weight of the Lancasters would be 70,000lbs, which
was 5,000lbs over the specified maximum for take-off.

Assuming they could get off the ground, a conventional approach by
two squadrons of Lancasters from across the North Sea would mean
an early warning for the target. The smokescreen and the fighters
would be up before any attackers could get there. If these problems
were solved, there remained the little local difficulty of actually hitting
the bullseye. Both Nos. 9 and 617 Squadrons were practising hard,
every day and night for what was to them still a mystery mission, but
the secret target, big as she was, wouldn't look so big from three or
four miles high. She was hugely powerful and heavily armoured. A

high-level attack would be necessary. This would give aircrew a better chance of survival against intensive shelling, and the bomb would have enough time to build up armour-piercing speed. Of course, the higher you flew, the tinier the ship looked in the bombsight.

Kåfjord was only 600 miles or so from Archangel. The plot was therefore hatched to send the boys to Russia. The two squadrons would fly to Scotland and top up on fuel, fly across the sea at night, bomb the *Tirpitz* soon after dawn, then carry on to an airfield near Archangel, a journey of well over 2,000 miles. They would recuperate in Russia, patch up their Lancasters, and fly home.

On 8 September, this plan was outlined to the two squadrons. Some of the Lancasters would be detailed to take the new, untried Johnny Walker mines, an ingenious, idiosyncratic and oh-so-British design which was actually classified as a bomb because it went off if it was dropped straight onto a solid object. Johnny Walker was a self-powered, roaming mine that was supposed to keep looking until it found its target. Lancaster crews didn't like it because it's self-power was a bottle of compressed hydrogen. Crews were under instruction to jettison their mines if they came under fighter or flak attack, which made them wonder what might happen in a dodgy landing or other out-of-the-ordinary, mine-jolting circumstance.

The bomb/mine had a parachute and an arming pin, both deployed by a fixed line as the weapon left the aircraft. It was extremely difficult to drop accurately but, in theory, this didn't matter too much. When it hit the water and automatically detached its chute, it sank to 50 or 60 feet, then, using its compressed hydrogen system, rose up again. If it didn't hit anything, for example the underside of *Tirpitz*, it sank again and 'walked' 30 feet to the side. To which side was anybody's guess. Up it rose again. If it missed again, it did another sink, walk and rise, wandering around at random until its gas ran out, whereupon it exploded, thus preventing German mine designers from finding it and having a good laugh. The Johnny Walker mine could only be deployed in deep water, like you have in a fjord, but don't have in normal harbours, canals and so on, where the shipping tends to be. It had never been used operationally before the *Tirpitz* raid. This was the novelty mine's chance to prove itself. Hopes among aircrew were not high.

Armaments officer Mick Maguire:

'If by some remote chance one of them had hit the *Tirpitz*, the armour plating would have shrugged it off. It had a very small charge. I thought they were a bloody waste of time and it would have been far better to have all the Lancs carrying Tallboys.'

In the event, weather changed the main plan. There was no point flying all the way to Kåfjord then finding cloud obscuring the target. Cloud was forecast, September was a cloudy month, so the revised scheme was to go straight to Russia, missing out Scotland, and wait there for the few hours of clear weather which must surely come along shortly. This decision was passed to Nos. 9 and 617 Squadrons around the middle of the day on 11 September 1944. Orders were to put together an overnight bag and take off at 1700 hours, land soon after dawn at an airfield on an island called Yagodnik in the river Dvina, and be prepared to attack the *Tirpitz* in the afternoon if the weather was right. Orders were orders. They'd had plenty of bombing and wind-finding practice over the last ten days. They were ready.

The task force initially consisted of twelve Lancasters from each squadron with Tallboys and six from each with a dozen Johnny Walker mines apiece, but No. 617 Squadron sent two extra Tallboy aircraft. Two unarmed B24 Liberators of No. 511 Squadron, Transport Command, carried the ground crews and the officer in charge of the op, Bardney station commander Group Captain McMullen and his staff for the operational HQ. There was also a Lancaster of No. 463 Squadron armed with cameras and a film crew, plus a Mosquito of No. 540 Squadron for reconnaissance and additional photographic duties. Altogether, there were almost 300 RAF personnel headed for Russia and the Arctic Circle. Mission: sink the *Tirpitz*.

The Liberators set off first from Bardney – they alone were going to Lossiemouth to top up with fuel before turning for Russia – then eighteen operational Lancasters led by No. 9 Squadron's CO, Wing Commander Bazin, plus the camera Lancaster.

'Puddle' Lake was in old faithful EE136 for the twenty-third and last time: Spirit of Russia on her way to the mother country. Alas, they hadn't flown very far before the Tallboy came adrift in the bomb bay. They had to jettison and come home. If the Spirit of Russia herself was not to be part of the *Tirpitz* attack, she was still well represented there by graduate pilots Tweddle, Jones, Scott and Stowell.

This epic adventure has been as well dissected and described as any raid could be in many books. In brief, after flights handicapped by every misfortune possible at that time, by a marvel, nineteen Lancasters landed safely at Yagodnik and eleven at nearby Kegostrov. The rest were in various states of disrepair at unscheduled and unsuitable places, some of which were outlandish even by local standards. Somehow over the next day, 13 September, all the crews were assembled, present, correct and unharmed, at Yagodnik, if not all their aircraft.

Not a single one of the Lancasters had been fit to operate as planned on the day they landed. The crews were exhausted and scattered in any case, but every aircraft needed work doing to it and, because of the late change of plan, ground crews and spare parts were not already there as they should have been. As if that were not enough, the refuelling arrangements were quite inadequate for this number of hungry big birds. Tanks said to contain 3,500 gallons were found to hold 350, and it would take most of a day before all the serviceable aircraft were filled.

For the next two days, frantic efforts were made to collect, repair and refit as many Lancasters as possible, and on 15 September, all were to attack the battleship, ten of No. 9 Squadron and seventeen of No. 617 Squadron, twenty altogether with Tallboys and the rest with Johnny Walker mines.

Most of the Tallboy aircraft flew in more or less directly astern of the battleship which, to the bomb aimers, looked about the size of a Swan Vesta. Not only were they three miles or so above her, but to hit from an aircraft flying at about 200 miles an hour they would have to release their bombs a mile and a half in advance. Over the target – something like twenty-five seconds later – flying much more slowly than the bomb was falling, on a clear day they would have been able to see if their own near-supersonic speck of a bomb had hit the matchstick. Clarity was in short supply as the Germans put up their smokescreens and filled the air with a barrage of flak and shellfire, including the heavy artillery. *Tirpitz*, the bomber crews saw, could defend herself very well indeed.

As it was, they bombed from various heights and all within thirteen minutes, sometimes aiming for a piece of the ship they could see, sometimes for her gun flashes in the midst of the smoke. Not surprisingly, some bombs fell in the water. The ex-EE136 crews reported thus, with Tweddle one of the first to bomb:

WS/U, F/O Tweddle; 10.56, 15,800 ft. *A large column of brown smoke rising from target.*

WS/P, F/O Jones; 11.00, 12,500 ft. (own) *Results not seen. One plume of smoke seen at estimated position of ship.*

WS/V, F/O Scott; *target not attacked. Tallboy would not release in spite of making four runs over target. It eventually fell off through bomb doors.*

Stowell had Johnny Walker mines. *Smoke screen obscured ship. About 20 JW mines fell in the fjord.*

Of the No. 617 Squadron crews, four had the JW mines, four did not bomb, while nine did drop their Tallboys, but none reported a hit of their own, only some near misses. The general opinion was that there had been one or perhaps two good hits. They didn't see it because of the smokescreen but No. 617 Squadron's Flight Lieutenant John Pryor and his bomb aimer, Pilot Officer Hoyland, missed by a whisker. The sound of their Tallboy, dropped at 1056 hours and exploding just off the starboard side, must have amplified the terrible shock and much louder bang of the single hitting bomb smashing through the foredeck, dropped at 1055 hours by the most frequent flyer of No. 9 Squadron's other centurion Lancaster, W4964 J-Johnny Walker, Flight Lieutenant Dougie Melrose, and bomb aimer Flying Officer Sammy Morris (see *Luck of a Lancaster* by this author).

For days after the raid, reports from Norwegian intelligence and intercepted German coded messages gave differing versions of the damage caused during Operation Paravane. In summary it seemed that the one hit had drilled through the foredeck at an angle and come out of the ship's hull near the waterline, before exploding some distance away. Had it exploded inside the ship it might well have sunk her.

Tirpitz was far more badly damaged than her attackers realised or the Germans would admit, except to themselves. A huge quantity of sea water – 1,500 tons – had flooded into a hole big enough to sail a boat through and *Tirpitz* had been reclassified by the Germans as u/s for war. Admiral Dönitz and a group of senior naval officers decided only a week after the raid that she was no longer fit for duty. She would need to sail to the fatherland for repairs and could only manage slow speeds, less than 10 knots, which would be a highly dangerous journey for her. Even then, it would be June 1945 before she could be ready to fight again, so it was thought that she could cause more short-term disruption to the Allied cause by doing the same as she had so far: hanging around in the fjords. As long as the Allies didn't find out what a mess she was in, they would continue to hop about in anxiety and tie up large resources in case their fears were realised.

Bomber Command mounted two more attacks on the *Tirpitz*, sinking her on the third, the raids not featuring EE136, but Ed Stowell and Doug Tweddle can claim the rarest distinction of being ex-WS/R skippers and flying on all three *Tirpitz* raids.

The emphasis returned to Germany, prioritised thus: oil installations, railways and vehicle factories, cities in general if the other types of target were not practicable. Beside all this ran the support of the ground forces in France and keeping the V weapons in check, plus any special targets which might be considered imperative from time to time. C-in-C Harris believed that Germany would implode if city bombing was resumed at full power, making a high-casualty invasion unnecessary. Other service chiefs wanted the oil and the transport knocked out so that the invasion would be less costly. The compromise meant that neither philosophy was fully tested.

Normal squadron service was resumed on 23 September. Full control of Bomber Command was back with C-in-C Harris after his summer of following Eisenhower's demands, although army support work would still be on the roster and No. 9 Squadron would be closely involved where great precision was needed. Some other things had changed, too. The Luftwaffe was no longer the power it was and, with the resources of Fighter Command much more at his disposal, Harris could order daylight raids with strong escorts. All the other risks remained, of course, and the flak was still there. You could never forget the flak.

First up was an evening raid, take off at seven, back at one, to the aqueduct near Münster on the Dortmund-Ems Canal. The canal was of the highest importance to the Germans and they had seen Bomber Command drain it several times. It would be breached again tonight, by a force including twelve of No. 9 Squadron (six with Tallboys), while eleven Tallboy aircraft of No. 617 Squadron – the squadron that had lost six Lancasters out of nine there only a year before – went to the built-up section at Ladbergen. Another ninety or so of other 5 Group squadrons went with 1,000lb bombs. A warm welcome was guaranteed; the Germans expected the bombers all the time and were ready.

The crews of No. 9 Squadron found ten-tenths cloud over the aqueduct target, down to 7,000 feet. Those with conventional loads bombed the canal banks on red TI's seen through the murk. The Tallboy carriers could not be so profligate and so turned for home. They were expensive things, Tallboy bombs. They were not allowed to waste them, even if landing with one was a hazard.

Tweddle was down with his Tallboy nine minutes after midnight, as were a couple of the conventionals. Future EE136 captain, Flying Officer W.G. Rees, who was on his second op, attacked by a fighter, hit by flak, landed at home on three engines at 0026 hours. At about that time, a night-fighter found LL901 WS/V-Victor, flown by Flight Lieutenant Charles Scott who, as a rookie pilot officer, had skippered WS/R twice way back in July when they were on their French trips.

He had clocked up twenty-eight ops including his second Dicky. Navigator, Flight Sergeant 'Curly' Harding and the rest of the crew were on twenty-seven, and V-Victor wanted one for her fifty. That was 23 September, when they were all killed – except the bomb aimer – in their crash in central Netherlands, about 70 miles from the coast. They were a week or two short; they had only managed three and a half months. On 23 October, Mrs Harding gave birth to son Michael, who became the well-known entertainer.

Sergeant Jim Brookbank was a recently arrived bomb aimer with another pilot called Scott:

'Our skipper Scotty, F/O W. Scott, wounded at Brest, was still convalescing. He and all of us were posted as killed instead of F/Lt C.B. Scott's crew. When the Service Police came to clear up our quarters and started taking our stuff, it was a stroke of luck that some of us 'dead' men were there, or the telegrams would surely have gone out to the wrong crew's families. A few days after that I was walking down Lincoln High Street and a lad I knew from training in Canada came up to me and asked me what I was doing there, seeing as I was dead. I said no I wasn't, which I thought was clear enough despite what had apparently been printed in the 5 Group news sheet.'

WS/R hosted another new crew for the railways and the engineering factories at Karlsruhe on 26 September, Australian Flying Officer R.W. Ayrton taking off at 0057 hours and expecting to be home in time for breakfast. It was cloudy. They dropped their bombs on the glow of fires already started, or on TIs dimly perceived. R-graduate Adams had his bombing interrupted. Report:

'Primary attacked 0400 hours, 11,500 ft. Bombed red TI but owing to combat on bombing run could not delay full 26 seconds.'

Straight and level flight on the bombing run usually meant a better target for the flak; in this case the mid-upper gunner, Frank Stebbings, spotted an Me410 approaching very fast on his starboard side. This twin-engined successor to the Me110 came in a variant with a 50mm (two-inch) cannon like the Panzer tanks carried, allowing the fighter to take pot shots at 1,000 yards. This very rarely worked, so the conventional Me410 with machine guns and 20mm cannon was more effective.

Stebbings ordered 'Corkscrew starboard' and swung his guns, as did Fred Whitfield in the rear turret. Exactly according to the book, the German aircraft sped over the top of them as they dived. Frank and Fred poured bullets into him and he broke away in flames. Nothing better, thought Fred and Frank.

It was bombing according to the book too. Despite the cloud, large areas of the city were destroyed for the loss of two Lancasters out of 226, and it was much the same at Kaiserslautern, a smaller target for the night of 27 September, a town of 70,000 in Bavaria with steelworks and the usual range of factories. Ayrton and crew in EE136 contributed to the destruction of one third of the built-up area (another third was already destroyed by the Americans). In a fairly flak-free zone they bombed from between 4,000 and 5,000 feet, and good fires were seen to be numerous, especially well concentrated around the church spire and, according to Ayrton, about half a mile east of the autobahn.

On a daylight to Wilhelmshaven on 5 October, the clouds were so thick it might as well have been the darkest night. New EE136 captain, Kiwi Flying Officer Waters, bombed blind on instructions from the controller, as did most of the others including R-old-boys Camsell, Ayrton and Newton, and Bradford's old crew flying now with Redfern in that other great old madame, W4964 WS/J-Johnny on her 106th op. Waters's flight engineer for the rest of the year, Sergeant Colin Booth, would swap with Cliff Newton's man for one fatal flight on New Year's Day 1945.

There was yet another new crew for EE136 to Bremen on 6 October, the last and most effective of more than thirty attacks on this city, including one of the famous thousand-bomber raids of 1942. With a three-quarter moon to guide them, 246 Lancasters destroyed approximately 5,000 houses and fifty factories; including some of the shipyards, the Focke-Wulf aircraft factories and Siemens electrical works, for the loss of five aircraft. It could have been more; 'Streets were seen by the light of the fires' (ORB) but the fires didn't spread as they might have because so much of Bremen was already laid flat. In any case, Bomber Command did not need to go there again.

A series of watery daylight targets followed for No. 9 Squadron; Dutch sea walls to be breached and a dam to be bust. The sea walls proved easier than the dam and were part of the plan to bomb the Germans out of their fortress at Walcheren Island. They were on the run everywhere else but here, at the mouth of the Scheldt, the route into Antwerp. The city was already in Allied hands but could not be used for urgently needed supplies because the Germans controlled the estuary from Walcheren, an 'island', most of which was below sea level.

They went for the dyke at Vlissingen (Flushing) over lunchtime on 7 October, bombing from around 6,000 feet with the 4,000lb cookie. Redfern saw water coming through the dyke; 'Puddle' Lake said his own bomb was seen to hit it and Keeley, back in EE136 for her ninetieth, saw the target definitely hit. The strategic value of this success was doubtful. The Germans were not flushed out, and the Canadian ground forces trying to evict them found that the flooding made their task more difficult.

Regardless of that, the squadron went again on 11 October, a three-hour trip, looking for the gun emplacements on the sea wall. EE136 now seemed to have become the Lancaster equivalent of a pool car with yet another different crew; the captain was Flying Officer Anderson, who couldn't see much through the cloud although others reported large explosions.

The Sorpe was one of the dams in the great No. 617 Squadron Dambusters raid; it was left to the last, not usefully damaged and kept the Ruhr supplied with water while the breached Möhne dam was rebuilt. At the time of the Dambusters raid, the Germans had speculated on what might have happened had the second dam on the list been the Sorpe rather than the Eder, the breach of which didn't affect the Ruhr. In fact, results almost certainly would have been no different.

On 15 October, eighteen Lancasters of No. 9 Squadron went to the Sorpe Dam with Tallboy bombs, escorted by almost sixty Mustangs. All the No. 617 Squadron skippers on that famous moonlit night had been very experienced; most were so on No. 9 Squadron's morning effort, but not all. Two aircraft were jostled by others over the target and as a result were unable to make an attack. Laws – an experienced pilot on squadron since July – was overtaken by another aircraft:

'I was driven off course to starboard and came over target on wrong heading, so bomb was not dropped.'

Redfern had the narrowest escape. He missed having a Tallboy through his wing by the very thinnest of toothskin:

'Target not attacked as aircraft directly above dropped bomb as own bomb aimer was about to get aiming point in the graticule. Turned own aircraft to starboard to avoid bomb which fell just ahead of port wing. Request made for another run but leader instructed to rejoin formation.'

Keeley, in his familiar seat in EE136, saw a crater but didn't know what his own bomb had done. There were nine hits and near misses, with one direct hit on the very crest of the dam, smack in the middle, making a large crater, but that was all the bombs made, craters, not holes. Accurate though the bombing was and in trying circumstances, the dam was proof against the Tallboy, being a thousand feet thick at its base with its concrete centre reinforced and protected by many, many feet of earth and rubble. Perhaps, had the Germans kept the water level as high as it had been pre-Dambusters, the extra pressure would have made a breach. More likely, the Sorpe would have stood, however many bombs hit it, bouncing, spinning or otherwise.

While two forces of 250+ Lancasters went to Stuttgart on the nineteenth, a similar one featuring No. 9 Squadron went to Nürnberg, hoping to finish off the blasted place. Large parts of the southern industrial districts were wrecked but it wasn't the blow they wanted, and that was that for EE136 Spirit of Russia, as Keeley brought her back to Bardney for the last time as WS/R-Robert, after ninety-three ops.

Chapter Eight

She Wasn't Done Yet

They painted out the WS/R and redid her with CA/R for No. 189 Squadron, being reformed in this month of October on the same station. Their first op featured EE136 CA/R, among five Lancasters to Homburg from Bardney on 1 November. These five were not all ancients, passed along to help out while No. 189 Squadron got its act together. Two more were from No. 9 Squadron, but mere youngsters compared to EE136, and two were brand new, both of which would soon be lost.

The target for the raid, 226 Lancasters altogether, was the Meerbeck oil refinery, but the marking was poor, the weather cloudy, and only two-thirds of the force attempted to bomb. The only bomber from No. 189 Squadron was EE136, captain Flying Officer D.M.S. Van Cuylenberg, ex No. 44 Squadron, who saw some TIs but no results, while the rest complained about no markers and radios being jammed by other Lancasters' transmissions.

Next day they relocated to Fulbeck, between Newark and Sleaford, previously an American base. The move involved twenty-nine officers, fifty NCO aircrew and 228 ground crew of all types and ranks. Instructions included:

'Officers and NCOs travelling by their private cars are to inform the Adjutant of their names before 1000 hours.'
'Clean working dress will be worn.'
'Seven Lancaster Aircraft will proceed by air.'

Flying Officer Brian had the privilege of taking CA/R and could look forward to one EE136 trip in anger and war-survival for him and his crew. Of the other six pilots proceeding by air – Flight Lieutenant Abbott and Flying Officers Blain, Davies, Kelly, Ryan and Van Cuylenburg – four would not last the winter, with three of them killed on the same night.

The new squadron's next effort was 6 November, six Lancasters going with 230 more to the junction of the Mittelland and Dortmund-Ems canals at Gravenhorst. Despite good visibility the marking was a mess and little bombing was done, while one of No. 189 Squadron spotted a new hazard:

'British searchlights shining right over the track, both from Brussels and Antwerp (which) gave the position of main force.'

EE136 didn't go on that one, but she was away on the eleventh, to Harburg with Flight Lieutenant Fred Abbott. It was an unusual crew in a way – the pilot was thirty, the navigator forty, the bomb aimer twenty, and one of the gunners was Belgian – and they would be EE136's most frequent flyers with No. 189 Squadron. The target was not the picturesque Bavarian village of Harburg but the eponymous southern suburb of Hamburg, where there was an oil refinery and a rubber factory. They missed the oil and the rubber and, as part of No. 189 Squadron's worst night, would have to go back.

The squadron was building up to full strength and could send twelve on a quite different kind of raid on 16 November, a daylight in preparation for an American ground advance. The soldiers' supplies of artillery shells were not getting through and so Bomber Command was required to clear the way by attacking three towns between Aachen and the Rhine – Düren, Heinsburg and Jülich, which all sat on the river Rur (Roer). EE136, on her ninety-sixth, was captained by Flying Officer

Brian, ex No. 61 Squadron like Abbott, and he reported concentrated bombing of Düren, 'town obliterated', as indeed it was, and as might have been expected when almost 500 Lancasters bombed a town of only 22,000 people in the middle of the day.

A long and bitter ground battle followed for the Hürtgenwald, with very large losses on both sides, superseded in importance and fame by the Battle of the Bulge, before the Americans at last crossed the Rur at Düren on 25 February 1945.

Pilot Officer Jack Coad reported from No. 44 Squadron as acting flying officer on 11 November, along with some of his old crew, all sergeants – engineer Boyson, navigator Dunville, and gunners Joyner and Powell. Sergeant Powell was an old stager from the biplane RAF of the 1920s, still going strong after all those years and destined for a rather spectacular end to his long career.

With No. 44 Squadron men augmented, Coad took EE136 to Munich on 26 November, a night when No. 189 Squadron suffered the first loss of this war, but without interference from the enemy. Lancaster PB745 took off at 2353 hours and crashed eleven minutes later at the village of Saltby, about 15 miles to the south-west of Fulbeck; four survived, three killed. Munich, according to Coad, went well.

Heilbronn, population about 80,000, was a prosperous manufacturing and business centre in south-west Germany, with a large inland port on the river Neckar. There had been several incidental bombings, including one by the Americans in September as a secondary target, but nothing could have prepared the citizens for the evening of 4 December.

Fred Abbott was skippering EE136, one of fifteen from the squadron joining another 270 Lancasters, taking off around 1640 hours and bombing in the second wave at 1940 hours. Several captains reported fighter activity over the target, one machine was lost of thirteen on the night, and Jack Coad had to land away from home due to a u/s Gee box and consequent fuel shortage, pilot's Perspex shattered by ice, mid-upper guns u/s, 'trip otherwise uneventful.'

Some 14,000 feet below Coad's humorous outlook, the bombers started a firestorm that completely destroyed the city centre and surrounding districts. The official estimate was four-fifths of the town laid waste. Thousands died in the fires, half the population fled, and Heilbronn was no more.

The grim work continued on the night of 6 December, at Giessen, ancient university town in Hesse, population 50,000, some factories, a brewery, an important railway junction, but not really the sort of place that would have been on the list in 1943. Abbott was in EE136 again, on her ninety-ninth, part of a force of 255 Lancasters that destroyed three-quarters of the town in a few minutes, with little opposition from flak although there were fighters about, and totally destroyed the railway yards.

When the one hundred ops came up for EE136, the target was the dam on the river Urft near Heimbach, southern Germany, not very far from the Belgian and Netherlands borders. This dam was built at the start of the twentieth century and held a reservoir that was the biggest in Europe at the time; it had the potential for disrupting Allied advances on the ground. To prevent the Germans releasing floodwaters at tactical moments, it was judged better to wreck the thing entirely, and this was the second of three attempts to do so. Some damage resulted but not sufficient.

Flying Officer Seddon, ex No. 207 Squadron, was in charge of the ton-up Lancaster, and his bomb aimer, Flight Sergeant Harry Hodder, did not have a happy time of it:

'Bombs did not go on bomb tit so endeavoured to get bombs on target by jettison action.'

They were all together again at Munich on 17 December, with railways and the old town centre as aiming points, and the general opinion matched the results: a very good raid. Munich was a long way, an eight-hour round trip but not so dangerous as it used to be, the night-fighters now being a much reduced threat due to lack of petrol and supplies. Still, six Lancasters went down out of 280, plus two not caused by enemy action, and life in Bomber Command remained precarious.

There was another long trip on 18 December to Gdynia. In 1924, Gdynia had been a little Polish fishing village on the Baltic near Danzig. Ten years later it had become one of the biggest harbours in Europe, sheltering the German pocket battleship *Lützow*, previously known as the *Deutchland*. After a patchy career and many technical troubles, the diesel-powered monster had been used for a year as a training ship. With *Tirpitz* gone, perhaps she might be re-enlisted in the cause, and so 236 Lancasters set out to sink her.

The pilots of No. 189 Squadron were instructed to make use of the automatic pilot, George, on the long haul over the sea, and many of them did, for eight hours or more. Jack Coad's experience of the operation allows an insight into the technology of the time:

'Marking very good. Smoke seen but snow and smoke made it (the battleship) difficult to identify visually. George engaged for twenty minutes, had to disengage as apparatus would not settle down. Kept climbing and diving. VHF found to be u/s and when w/op fitted new fuse it blew again.'

Fred Abbott used George for four hours in EE136 and had no bother, but nobody hit the *Lützow* and there were several more attempts until No. 617 Squadron hit her with a Tallboy and sunk her in shallow water, where she remained as a gun battery against the Red Army.

Pressure had increased on C-in-C Harris to reduce Germany's fuel supplies still further. Some of the oil facilities made remote targets, beyond the range of Oboe and Gee, so, Harris argued, good weather would be needed to reach refineries such as Leuna and Pölitz which, of course, would also favour the defenders. He had to give in eventually and losses proved surprisingly light. Taking off on 21 December for Pölitz, Abbott, in EE136, was one of a force of over 200 Lancasters of which four down could be ascribed to enemy action, two of them from No. 189 Squadron.

'Light' losses meant lighter than before, lighter than in the nights of 1943 and 1944 when the Luftwaffe was a mighty force. There would still be losses in 1945.

For off-duty aircrew, every night was party night. Eat and drink for tomorrow we die. Even so, there was a special atmosphere about New Year's Eve, 1944. Most people hoped and many expected that this year coming would be the last of the war in Europe. Everyone lucky enough to be on leave, whether confined to the pleasure domes of an RAF base, or not, celebrated to the utmost.

Those crews of ten Lancasters of No. 9 Squadron whose names were on the battle order for take-off at 0745 hours on 1 January, had to keep to a modest few beers and get to bed in good time, knowing that their alarm clock, a Service Policeman, would be shaking them at three in the morning to go to briefing and asking them to sign his clipboard to confirm that they had indeed been woken as prescribed.

Bomber Command was now an extremely effective and powerful force. Butch Harris was by no means alone in thinking that, if the invasion faltered or was repelled, the RAF on its own could render Germany incapable of further resistance. Von Rundstedt had opened his counter attack in the Ardennes on 16 December, the Battle of the Bulge, greatly aided at first by a long period of bad flying weather, fog and low cloud. A year before, the Wehrmacht Field Marshal Keitel had said that the strength of the Allies lay chiefly in their air force, and von Rundstedt knew that his hopes of turning back the invaders rested to an extent on the luck of the weather.

By late December, his luck had run out. Bomber attacks on roads and railways had prevented or decisively slowed troop movements and were a key factor in the swift breakdown of the offensive. Panther and Tiger tanks were brilliant fighting machines but bombing had brought tank production to a level far below what was wanted. Fuel was desperately short because of the raids on refineries and synthetic oil plants, so that many of the tanks never got to the battlefield, or were very restricted in what they could do if they did arrive.

Attacks on the means of production and distribution remained a high priority and the Dortmund-Ems canal had once again appeared at the top of the list. So essential was it to the German system that every possible resource was always put into repairing it. It seemed that no matter what the bombers did, the Germans and their slave labour could nullify their efforts in short order and get the ships floating again along this vital highway of war.

New Year's Eve into New Year's Day was a very cold night, one of a series of cold nights. As usual in the Nissen huts, the coke stoves had been stoked up and given full draught until they were glowing red and, as usual, they had gone out soon afterwards. The men who liked a glass of water by their beds found it frozen over in the morning. Only those who wore their inner flying suits or other such insulation over their pyjamas could lie in their beds without shivering.

It was perishing, frosty and black dark as the crews were taken to their dispersals at around 0645 hours and it was still dark when, second in line at 0747 hours, EE136 graduate Cliff Newton surged down the runway in the new WS/R-Robert, NG252, six ops so far. He took to the air with almost the same crew as always, the men who had flown in the old R, Spirit of Russia, to the U-boat pens at La Pallice way back in the summer. The 'almost' was a change in flight engineer, Waters' regular man Sergeant Booth filling in for this show, but he was an EE136 graduate too.

As the third Lancaster took its place at the head of the runway, engines revving hard against the brakes, waiting for the green light, there was a huge Wooomph! and a great flash of fire some distance away. Everyone thought some poor sod at Woodhall had gone in. Woodhall Spa, base for No. 617 Squadron, was six or seven miles away, but the explosion in fact was much nearer home. Once up, Newton's engines had cut and the Lancaster, fully loaded, powerless when it needed power the most, had crashed into a field. The pilot and five of his crew were killed in the fire. Another founder member, the bomb aimer, Pilot Officer Paddy Flynn, was thrown clear and escaped with injuries. The cause of failure was never finally resolved, but frozen water in the fuel seemed the most likely possibility.

Along the Atlantic coast were several German pockets of resistance, blocking access to ports and the French hinterland, the most southerly of which was Royan/La Pointe de Grave, which prevented American access to the Gironde and Bordeaux. Laying siege to Royan was a less than ideal collection of the only troops available, who were mostly ex-Resistance fighters, now called *Forces Françaises de L'Intérieur* (FFI), aided by a small unit of American artillery and led by Resistance officers who had no background in 'proper' warfare. It was a stand-off between the poorly equipped and inexperienced many outside, versus the determined and professional few inside the town.

Among the French besiegers were also the post-liberation rivalries and suspicions, and, to top it all, a hard winter was making provisioning very difficult for both sides.

The German commander gave permission for the civilian population to leave; about 8,000 went but 2,000 stayed. These 2,000 were variously described by Allied interests as collaborators or not there at all, and by the time the orders reached Bomber Command, via French and American officers on the ground, via SHAEF (Supreme Headquarters Allied Expeditionary Force), the mission was to destroy a town occupied by German troops only.

It is possible that SHAEF had second thoughts about the civilians in the town, but no cancellation was received to the orders that apparently reached Bomber Command from SHAEF-Air at noon on 4 January, that the raid should take place the following night. It seems that this was interpreted as the night immediately following, tonight, and the attackers took off around 2400 hours.

Those who believed in luck might have wondered if keeping the Spirit of Russia going for so long was such a good idea after all. Eighteen were sent by No. 189 Squadron to Royan; EE136 was on her 104th op with her fortieth crew aboard, led by Flying Officer Sidney Reid and the only CA/R old boys on the trip were Coad and co.

The squadron's contingent all bombed at around 0405 hours, part of a second wave going in an hour after the first. This meant that there were a lot of people on the streets, German and French alike, thinking the raid was over, trying to rescue the injured and recover the dead.

The total from the two attacks was 442 French civilians killed, several hundreds more wounded, and forty-seven German soldiers dead. The town held a large funeral procession. Someone who witnessed it described what he saw:

'I will never forget this man, the sole survivor of his aircraft. This aviator, in battledress and flying boots, with a white pullover hanging down to his thighs, bare headed, followed the last of the convoy of open-topped military trucks, with the rest of the cortege behind him. He carried the burden of mourning for his comrades and he wept.'

This man was Sergeant Powell, Coad's rear gunner. A few minutes after bombing, heading for home, his crewmates had been killed in a mid-air collision over Cognac with a No. 467 Squadron Lancaster, all of whose crew got out. Among the dead were Jack Coad's No. 44 Squadron originals, Geoffrey Boyson and Joseph Dunhill. Regular bomb-aimer Sergeant Joyner was on leave and so Harry Hodder, regular with Seddon, had filled in.

Most of the remaining civilians left the Royan pocket, after a ten-day truce, while searches went on for survivors in the rubble. What was left of the town, about 20 per cent of its buildings, was surrendered by the Germans on 17 April.

There followed some large, 'old-fashioned' raids – in round numbers, 700 Lancasters and Halifaxes to Hannover, 500 to Hanau, and 650 to Munich, including EE136 on 7 January. Yet another new skipper, Flying Officer J.S. Penning, reported, 'attack widespread but successful' and that was the last big one for Munich to suffer. Penning and his men had some of R-Robert's luck; they finished the war intact.

The U-boat pens at Bergen were a joint effort by No. 9 Squadron and No. 617 Squadron, with Tallboys on 12 January. Among those going were Flight Sergeant Bradford's crew, who had been to those other U-boat pens at La Pallice in EE136 in August, and had been taken over by Flying Officer Ernie Redfern, a pilot on No. 9 Squadron since May.

The Mark 14A sight that No. 9 Squadron used allowed them to bomb on offset marking and a false wind, which overcame some of the obscuring effects of smoke over the target. The SABS sight, used by No. 617 Squadron, required visual target ID and so they would go in first.

There had been two raids by Lancasters the previous October, featuring a total of 284 aircraft with only four losses, but with ordinary bombs they hadn't stood much chance of making a serious mark on the place. They had sunk four U-boats in the harbour and some other shipping, but they had also managed to drop bombs on the town, killing many Bergen citizens.

The enemy fighter stations were equipped with the Me210 and Me410, but these, Intelligence at Bardney said, would be snowbound. This was all cheering news, although the previous raids were at night and this was going to be at lunchtime. Intelligence at Woodhall Spa had a different opinion on fighters. Here, the officer said that there were two FW190 *staffeln* based at Herdla, north of Bergen and strong fighter opposition could be expected. Nobody told No. 9 Squadron.

On a sunny morning they took off from 0830 hours onwards. The aim was to bomb at 1300 hours and be home in time for tea. A fighter escort of Mustangs, thirteen aircraft of No. 315 (Polish) Squadron under Squadron Leader Anders, plus two Mosquitos of No. 169 Squadron were to pick up the four flights of bombers near Peterhead and stay with them over the target. There would also be an Air-Sea Rescue Warwick.

Three hours drummed along over the North Sea on a sparkling clear day and here they were, looking down on the U-boat pens. There was plenty of flak, both the light and the heavy kinds. There was more of the light, the tracer, but it was especially unnerving on daylights being able to see the heavy flak exploding so clearly, those innocent looking puffs of smoke which could blow your wing off. The Americans, who flew in strict formation at a standard height on their mass daylight raids, said that when you were flying through flak, you could watch the patterns in the puffs and work out when it was going to be your turn to get it.

The Polish Mustangs turned up at last, their pilots becoming anxious about the amount of flak to which their bombers were being subjected and thinking they had better do something about it. Possibly they didn't realise how long the raid might go on and how long the Lancasters could be hanging around trying to bomb in the smoke and haze. Possibly they had had the same briefing as No. 9 Squadron: no enemy fighters expected. In any case, they concluded that there was nothing more productive they could do than shoot up the ack-ack, so down they went.

This might have been jolly good fun for the cavalry, but not so much for the heavy mob, which was beginning to feel collectively nervous about a large number of tiny dots in the sky speeding towards them with ferocious intent.

Down below, the Mustang pilots were having a great time, killing Germans and taking revenge for their national tragedies of 1939. Not surprisingly, having forgotten their original purpose and now going hammer and tongs at the enemy, the Poles didn't notice that their British colleagues were under threat many thousands of feet above. Several of the Lancaster skippers ordered Very lights to be fired from the signal pistol, which was fixed aft of the astrodome, angled backwards, behind the wireless operator's position. The idea was that a red flare might catch the Poles' attention. Even if the ploy worked, the Mustangs still had a long way to climb before they could be any use against the German fighters.

Four times EE136 captain, Les Keeley, saw two Lancasters being attacked and said the fighter escort did not go to their assistance. Another No. 9 Squadron skipper reported:

'We were attacked by five FW190s who peeled off in turn and the attacks went on consistently from 1309 to 1327hrs. We ended up at 900 feet with 360mph on the clock after corkscrewing continuously. After seeing the fighter escort at the concentration (assembly point, Scottish coast) we never saw them again except for one which stood off and watched us near the end of the attacks. One Lancaster was seen to be shot down on fire and to go straight into the sea.'

A No. 9 Squadron bomb aimer, Dennis Nolan, saw that too, but there was a more dramatic edge from his point of view:

'Our Lancaster and another were flying on a similar course, but the other was about two thousand feet lower, and we had three more aircraft in our view, which were FW190s. They stooged about while we watched them make up their minds. They were choosing. The sods were selecting which bomber to go for, us or him. They chose him. He corkscrewed and appeared to be getting free when one of his engines caught fire, and then another. That Lanc hit the sea in a way which clearly said to us, watching from above, that there could be no survivors, but the fighters carried on shooting into the burning wreckage until they had no ammunition left. They couldn't attack any more Lancasters, such as ours for example, so they flew away. I thought that here were three of the best fighter aircraft of the war, operated by three of the worst or least experienced pilots.'

The Lancaster that Nolan and most of the squadron saw falling in flames into the sea was NG257 WS/N, belonging to Flying Officer Ernest Cyril Redfern, DFC, aged twenty-two, recently married to Frances. Bergen was his fortieth op. He hadn't flown in EE136; his crew had, but they were all dead just the same.

There was to be a stand-down for 5 Group over the last two weeks of January, but before that were two trips for EE136 with another new No. 189 Squadron crew, led by Flying Officer Pat Glenville, late of No. 50 Squadron. They went to the Pölitz oil facility and smashed it in fair weather. Glenville thought it was 'a good, clear target well marked' but, perhaps explaining a less than perfect photograph, complained that his aircraft, R-Robert on her 106th, had been on fire on the bombing run and was flying with the port wing low.

All damage was repaired between homecoming at 0300 hours and take-off at 1629 hours for the Merseburg/Leuna synthetic oil and chemical works. It was a highly successful raid, although Glenville thought the marking very scattered and did not consider it a good effort. Stanley Reid reported: 'One short combat just before reaching target. No claim. Another E/A attacked after leaving target but was lost in corkscrew.'

The last two ops for EE136 CA/R were with old friends Fred Abbott and crew, with that lucky bomb aimer Sergeant Joyner filling in as mid-upper gunner for the Belgian Jean Oberneck. The railways at Siegen were the target for op number 108, but the target was largely missed, and so to Karlsruhe on 2 February, the worst night of the war for No. 189 Squadron, which lost four Lancasters and crews. Three went down over Germany; in every case the rear gunner was the only survivor and the fourth crashed in France on the way home with the bomb aimer Flight Sergeant Blencowe surviving and, remarkably, rear gunner Sergeant Powell.

This was the same Sergeant Powell who had parachuted after Royan, taken part in the funerals there, somehow managed to make his way from the German-held pocket into liberated France, got himself back to Blighty and to his squadron at Fulbeck, put himself down for duty and, on his first op since then, had to parachute again hardly a month after the first time.

For him the war was over, and likewise for Lancaster Mark III EE136 WS/CA/R-Robert, the Spirit of Russia. Although Abbot did not report any special damage suffered on the last trip, almost two years of bomber war had caught up with the old girl and she was classified as Category E/FB, which is to say a write-off (E) due to operational loss (FB). While so many Lancasters had become FB in one moment, EE136 had 109 operations' worth of wear and tear.

The war, alas, was not over for some of CA/R's crews. The boys of No. 189 Squadron went to Ladbergen, Pölitz, the infamous Dresden raid, all without loss; the oil refinery at Rositz, near Leipzig, where one Lancaster was lost with all hands; Böhlen, and Gravenhorst on 21 February. This was yet another attempt to breach the Mittelland Canal, and in clear weather they did it, but at a cost. It was a smallish force, only 165 Lancasters, but thirteen went down, 8 per cent.

Pat Granville and crew had been on leave. Their regular bomb aimer, Flying Officer Hammersley, still wasn't back when they were on the battle order to go to Gravenhorst in NG321 CA/V-Victor, so newcomer, Pilot Officer Trevor Perry, went with them on his second op. They fell near the target; all killed except mid-upper gunner Flight Sergeant Nolan.

In her absence, EE136's version of luck continued. Statistics tell lies, of course, but believers in fortune will point to a simple fact. With No. 189 Squadron, EE136 flew sixteen ops with eight different crews, and of those eight, four were shot down in other Lancasters, or 50 per cent. Maybe they should have retired the Spirit of Russia at No. 9 Squadron.

The next to go were Canadian Sid Reid and his men, all ex EE136. They'd been to Ladbergen on the night of 3/4 March, one of twelve from the squadron, 212 Lancasters altogether, trying to knock down that aqueduct again on the Dortmund-Ems Canal. They'd certainly helped to do that, with a double breach making the canal u/s for some time.

One No. 189 Squadron Lancaster came home early with engine trouble, one was shot down over the target, and NG325 CA/H was sixty miles from home, flying over some of the flatter and more rural parts of Norfolk, when she was spotted.

Reid could not have known that tonight was *Unternehmen* (Operation) *Gisela*, when around 200 night-fighters assembled over eastern England to raid airfields and catch the bombers on their way back. There were 550 such bombers to catch, Lancasters and Halifaxes, returning from missions in Germany, including some from training units that had been sent on a diversionary raid. There were others out on duty too, mine-laying for example, plus all the normal activity of night-flying exercises.

Some of the raiders flew in as far north as Scarborough; the southernmost crossed the Essex coast. Eight Lancasters and a Mosquito had been lost away on their operations, leaving ample returning supplies of unsuspecting victims, plus those out on training flights. The conversion units and OTUs took full crews on such travels and were wary, but didn't really expect to see anything to shoot at. The night-fighter threat was much reduced in any case, and raiders over home ground were a rarity, we might almost say forgotten about.

German pilots reported airfields with landing lights on and bomber aircraft with navigation lights ablaze. In about an hour, the raiders shot down twenty aircraft over Norfolk and Lincolnshire. Although the Germans lost a similar number later, mostly due to crashes through engine trouble or petrol shortage on the way back to base, only three, all Ju88s, are known to have been shot down over the UK.

One of the twenty bombers had Reid and crew inside. Still perhaps twenty minutes from home, the Lancaster had its nav lights on as it flew over RAF West Raynham, a substantial pre-war aerodrome about ten miles north-west of Dereham. Staff there who, by then, must have known there were intruders about, saw it, then saw the colours of the day being fired off, then heard cannon-fire. At 0118 in the morning of 4 March, two or three miles on from West Raynham, the Lancaster smashed into the little railway station just south of the village of East Rudham, on the line that took Midlanders to their holidays at Great Yarmouth and Cromer.

Next night the target was the oil refinery at Böhlen, not far from Leipzig, and that went well enough, but Harburg, going back to the oil and rubber there, was another disaster for No. 189 Squadron. They sent sixteen; four failed to return, among which was NG417 CA/P with Flight Lieutenant Frederick Abbott and all his crew killed as they fell near Visselhövede, about thirty miles south-west of the aiming point.

The four other EE136-veteran crews of No. 189 Squadron, those of Van Cuylenburg, Brian, Seddon and Penning, could consider themselves lucky to get through with a squadron that, considering its short lifespan – much less than year of active service – seemed to have suffered disproportionately.

The aircraft they'd all flown, classified as lost, was not entirely so. After a brief stay at a maintenance unit, the Spirit of Russia was flown to Cranwell and the Radio School that was previously the pre-First World War Royal Engineers Signals School, as an instructional airframe.

As technology developed, even that use ceased to be relevant and the last of EE136 was as a practice fire hulk at the RAF School of Fire Fighting, Sutton on Hull, in 1954.

Appendix

All the men of Lancaster Mark III EE136

The crews are listed in standard order: pilot, flight engineer, navigator, bomb aimer, wireless operator, mid–upper gunner, rear gunner.

No. 9 Squadron

1. J.H. Lyon, K. Pack, R.W. Corkill, H.W.E. Jeffery, A. Fielding, A.G. Denyer, G. Clegg. Also F.L. Chipperfield, navigator; C.J. Houbert, gunner (see crews 3 and 8).
2. J. Evans, V.G.L. Smith, R. Borthwick, V.J. Tarr, T. Myerscough, H.I. Ashdown, D.W. Brough.
3. W.W.W. Turnbull, J. Wellings, J. Waterhouse, J. McMasters, B. Owen, J. Michael, C.H. Bolt. Also F.L. Chipperfield, navigator; C.J. Houbert, gunner; Sergeant Lyon, wireless operator.
4. J. Livingstone, F. Parsons, F.T. Watson, H.C. Brewer, J. Prendergast, R.N. Browne, T.C. Taylor.
5. C. Payne, C.A. Gilbert, K.W. Armstrong, S.C. Young, J.B. Robinson, N.D. Bennett, P.A.S. Twinn.
6. K. Painter, T. Deacon, R.C. Saunders, J.E. Bacon, T. Andrews, S.P. Hone, D.W. Angell.
7. W. English, N.H. Mitchell, J.E. Evans, L.V. Fussell, L.G. Lane, D.R. Carlile, P.W.R. Hewitt.
8. J. McCubbin, N.D. Owen, B.J. Sherry, K.J. Dagnall, A.M. Smith, C.J. Houbert, J.L. Elliott.

9. W.E. Siddle, A.R. Wilson, M.C. Wright, N. Machin, J.W. Culley, J.C. Parker, C.C. Moore (see crew 14). Also J.W. Hearn, navigator; C.A. Peak, second pilot (see crew 15); S.G. Greenwood, navigator (see crew 14); R.T.C. Lodge, navigator; E. Singer, navigator.

10. H. Blow, F.S. Colman, S.W.A. Hurrell, H.P. Smith, R.O. Smith, R. Hartley, W.E. Miller.

11. W.J. Chambers, W.E. Haywood, W.J. Beeston, J.J. Hannon, I.M. Mulcuck, A.L. Steward, J.J. Campbell.

12. J.G.R. Ling, L. Moss, H. Laws, T. Fletcher, E.A. Gauld, E.J. Rush, I. Prada. Also J.N. Carter, navigator; H. Wood, gunner.

13. R.W. Mathers, A. Ball, T.A. Cave, W.E. Pearson, J.R. Donaldson, R.R. Nightingale, A.F. Bartlett. Also J. Thomas, flight engineer; D.A. Keeble, bomb aimer; W. Wilson, gunner; H.F. Robinson, gunner; W. Bingham, gunner; C.W. Howe, flight engineer.

14. L.G. Hadland, A.W. Cherrington, S.G. Greenwood, C.R. Brown, J. Gaskell, A.D. Tirel, C.C. Moore. Also N.C. Pleasance, passenger.

15. C.A. Peak, E.W. Kindred, T.W. Varey, E.J. Wilkes, W.V. Torbett, J.W. Nelson, J. Hogan.

16. H. Forrest, A.W. Hutton, S. Harwood, R.D. Hassall, D. Macauley, F.M. Corssman, D.B. Pinchin. Also J. Michael, gunner.

17. R.C. Lake, R.W. Baird, J.A. Peterson, G.B. Watts, G.E. Parkinson, S.G.D.L. Major, R.D. Kerr. Also D. McDonald, gunner; J.R. Gunnee, flight engineer.

18. L.J. Wood, T.M. Gordon, N. Oates, L.R. Lutwyche, D.G. Mumford, N. Hannah, J.E. Shuster.

19. G.A. Langford, C.G. Fenn, J.L. Wright, S.M. Mitchell, I. Feldman, J. Wright, G.T. Baseden.

20. C.B. Scott, J.E. Simkin, L.A. Harding, L.W. Langley, E.M. Hayward, F.A. Saunders, L.J. Hambly.

21. W.J. Sheppard, R. Johnstone, J.G. Glashan, J. Mulhearn, W.J. Toomey, W.J. Harris, B.S. Dean.

22. E.H.M. Relton, F.W. Johnson, C.H. Edwards, J.K. Scott, C.T. Scott, D.W. McConville, W.R. Andrew.

23. W.D. Tweddle, C.G. Heath, E. Shields, J. W. Singer, A. Carson, J.A. Foot, K. Mallinson.

24. R.F. Adams, L.A. Brown, H.R. Lynam, P.F. Jackson, R.F. Faucheux, F. Stebbings, F. Whitfield.

25. G.C. Camsell, W. Andrews, P.R. Aslin, R.H. Thomas, D. Beevers, W.J. Hebert, A.E. Boon.

26. J.E. Stowell, C.R. Spalding, J.G. Taylor, R.S. Liversedge, F. Millington, R.G. Bicker, M.W.A. Allsopp.

27. C.S. Newton, W. Gregory, P. Grant, R.C. Flynn, L.G. Kelly, E.H. Cooper, R.S. Stevens.

28. S.F. Bradford, J.W. Williams, R.W.R. Cooper, A.P. Hull, L.G. Roberts, W. Brand, D. Winch.

29. A.F. Jones, A.E.W. Biles, S. Scott, R.L. Blunsdon, R.L. Birch, R. Glover.

30. A. Keeley, A.E. Wotherspoon, W. Chorny, L.W. Tanner, S.D. Chambers, C.H. Cornwell, J.E. Johnson.

31. R.W. Ayrton, H.K. Huddlestone, M.J. Herkes, N. Bardsley, W. Scott, D.K. Chalcraft, J.A.W. Davies.

32. W.G. Rees, H. Mayhew, G.A. Hammond, D.A. Macintosh, T.A. Morrow, W.L. King, G.M. Heppell.

33. E.I. Waters, C. Booth, R. Miles, S. Coxon, E. French, G. Jones, W.T.G. Gabriel.

34. H. Anderson, W.D. Loakes, A.B. Vivian, E. Sumner, A. Cornfoot, K.A. Ashworth, G.M. Young.

No. 189 Squadron

35. D.M.S. Van Cuylenburg, G.H. Thompson, A.C.R Hayes, M.E. Goodhand, F.W. Ostopovich, K. Pursehouse, A.E. Smith.

36. F.J. Abbott, H. Henderson, J.F. Charlton, J.P. Rowan, W. Ashford, J.C. Oberneck, W.R. Kennedy. Also K. White, gunner; J. Gilmour, second pilot; E. Holdsworth, navigator; S.J. Joyner, gunner (see crew 38).
37. A.D.D. Brian, L.C. Doyle, L.W. Deubert, C. Morgan, L.W.H. Lambert, J.D. Constable, D.C. Wainwright.
38. J.I. Coad, G.A.T. Boyson, J.C. Dunville, M. Hislop, M. Browne, S.J. Joyner, R. Powell.
39. L.V. Seddon, J.A. Skilton, L.A. Lawrence, H.B. Hodder, W. Helliker, A. Tutill, G. White. Also J.H. Sands, flight engineer.
40. S.J. Reid, F.N. Benson, T.J. Nelson, H.G. Harrison, R.W. McCormack, G.F. Caley, M.R. Bullock.
41. J.S. Penning, A.E. Veitch, H. Loggin, R.B. Revill, A.G. Denyer, W. Langmaid, J. Brown.
42. P. Glenville, F. Pallister, L.S. Harper, D.B. Hammersley, C.J. Gallagher, J.L. Nolan, L. Moore.

All The Ops

Dates given are when the operations began. Names are of pilot-captains with ranks at the time. DNCO – Duty Not Carried Out. The usual reason was an early return forced by technical trouble or bad weather. DNCO ops counted for the aircraft but not for the crews.

1943

No. 9 Squadron

1.	11 June	Düsseldorf	Sergeant Lyon
2.	12 June	Bochum DNCO	Pilot Officer Evans
3.	14 June	Oberhausen	Sergeant Lyon
4.	8 July	Cologne	Sergeant Lyon

5.	9 July	Gelsenkirchen	Sergeant Lyon
6.	12 July	Turin	Sergeant Turnbull
7.	27 July	Hamburg	Flight Sergeant Livingstone
8.	29 July	Hamburg	Sergeant Payne
9.	30 July	Remscheid	Sergeant Lyon
10.	2 August	Hamburg DNCO	Pilot Officer Painter
11.	7 August	Milan	Flight Sergeant Lyon
12.	9 August	Mannheim	Sergeant Turnbull
13.	10 August	Nürnberg	Flight Sergeant Lyon
14.	12 August	Milan DNCO	Sergeant Turnbull
15.	14 August	Milan	Sergeant Turnbull
16.	15 August	Milan	Flight Sergeant Lyon
17.	17 August	Peenemünde	Flight Sergeant Lyon
18.	22 August	Leverkusen	Sergeant Turnbull
19.	27 August	Nürnberg	Pilot Officer Lyon
20.	30 August	Rheydt	Flying Officer English
21.	31 August	Berlin	Flying Officer English
22.	3 September	Berlin	Pilot Officer Lyon
23.	5 September	Mannheim	Pilot Officer McCubbin
24.	10 November	Modane	Pilot Officer Siddle
25.	18 November	Berlin	Pilot Officer Blow
26.	22 November	Berlin	Pilot Officer Chambers
27.	23 November	Berlin DNCO	Pilot Officer Ling
28.	26 November	Berlin	Pilot Officer Ling
29.	20 December	Frankfurt	Pilot Officer Ling
30.	23 December	Berlin	Pilot Officer Siddle
31.	29 December	Berlin	Pilot Officer Siddle

1944

| 32. | 1 January | Berlin | Pilot Officer Mathers |
| 33. | 5 January | Stettin | Pilot Officer Siddle |

34.	14 January	Brunswick	Pilot Officer Siddle
35.	20 January	Berlin	Flight Lieutenant Hadland
36.	21 January	Magdeburg	Flight Sergeant Peak
37.	27 January	Berlin	Flight Sergeant Peak
38.	28 January	Berlin	Flying Officer Mathers
39.	15 February	Berlin	Flying Officer Mathers
40.	19 February	Leipzig	Flying Officer Mathers
41.	20 February	Stuttgart	Flying Officer Mathers
42.	24 February	Schweinfurt	Pilot Officer Forrest
43.	1 March	Stuttgart	Pilot Officer Forrest
44.	9 March	Marignane	Flying Officer Mathers
45.	15 March	Stuttgart	Flying Officer Mathers
46.	22 March	Frankfurt	Flying Officer Mathers
47.	24 March	Berlin	Flying Officer Mathers
48.	21 May	Duisburg	Pilot Officer Lake
49.	22 May	Brunswick	Pilot Officer Lake
50.	27 May	Nantes	Pilot Officer Lake
51.	31 May	Saumur	Pilot Officer Lake
52.	3 June	Ferme d'Urville	Pilot Officer Lake
53.	6 June	Argentan	Pilot Officer Lake
54.	8 June	Rennes	Pilot Officer Lake
55.	12 June	Poitiers	Pilot Officer Lake
56.	14 June	Aunay-sur-Odon	Pilot Officer Lake
57.	15 June	Châtellerault	Pilot Officer Lake
58.	21 June	Gelsenkirchen	Pilot Officer Lake
59.	23 June	Limoges	Pilot Officer Wood
60.	24 June	Prouville	Pilot Officer Lake
61.	27 June	Vitry-le-François	Pilot Officer Wood
62.	4 July	St-Leu-d'Esserant	Pilot Officer Langford
63.	7 July	St-Leu-d'Esserant	Pilot Officer Scott

64.	12 July	Culmont-Chalindrey	Flying Officer Lake
65.	15 July	Nevers	Flying Officer Lake
66.	18 July	Caen	Flying Officer Sheppard
67.	19 July	Thierny	Flying Officer Lake
68.	20 July	Courtrai	Flying Officer Lake
69.	24 July	Donges	Flight Lieutenant Relton
70.	26 July	Givors DNCO	Flying Officer Lake
71.	28 July	Stuttgart	Flying Officer Lake
72.	30 July	Cahagnes	Flying Officer Scott
73.	31 July	Joigny	Flying Officer Tweddle
74.	1 August	Mont Candon	Flying Officer Lake
75.	2 August	Bois de Cassan	Flying Officer Lake
76.	3 August	Trossy	Flying Officer Adams
77.	11 August	Givors	Flight Lieutenant Camsell
78.	13 August	Brest	Flying Officer Lake
79.	14 August	Brest	Flying Officer Lake
80.	15 August	Gilze Rijen	Flight Sergeant Stowell
81.	16 August	La Pallice	Flying Officer Newton
82.	18 August	La Pallice	Flight Sergeant Bradford
83.	24 August	Ijmuiden	Flying Officer Jones
84.	27 August	Brest	Flight Sergeant Keeley
85.	11 September	Tirpitz DNCO	Flying Officer Lake
86.	26 September	Karlsruhe	Flying Officer Ayrton
87.	27 September	Kaiserslautern	Flying Officer Ayrton
88.	5 October	Wilhelmshaven	Flying Officer Waters
89.	6 October	Bremen	Flying Officer Rees
90.	7 October	Flushing	Flying Officer Keeley
91.	11 October	Flushing	Flying Officer Anderson
92.	15 October	Sorpe Dam	Flying Officer Keeley
93.	19 October	Nürnberg	Flying Officer Keeley

No. 189 Squadron

94.	1 November	Homburg	Flying Officer Van Cuylenburg
95.	11 November	Harburg	Flight Lieutenant Abbott
96.	16 November	Düren	Flying Officer Brian
97.	26 November	Munich	Flying Officer Coad
98.	4 December	Heilbronn	Flight Lieutenant Abbott
99.	6 December	Giessen	Flight Lieutenant Abbott
100.	8 December	Urft Dam	Flying Officer Seddon
101.	17 December	Munich	Flying Officer Seddon
102.	18 December	Gdynia	Flight Lieutenant Abbott
103.	21 December	Pölitz	Flight Lieutenant Abbott

1945

104.	4 January	Royan	Flying Officer Reid
105.	7 January	Munich	Flying Officer Penning
106.	13 January	Pölitz	Flying Officer Glenville
107.	14 January	Merseburg (Leuna)	Flying Officer Glenville
108.	1 February	Siegen	Flight Lieutenant Abbott
109.	2 February	Karlsruhe	Flight Lieutenant Abbott

Roll of Honour

Aircraft: Avro Lancaster of Nos. 9 and 189 Squadrons except where stated. Airmen noted here who did not fly in EE136 are marked.* Dates shown are those on which the operations began; actual dates of deaths cannot always be reliably ascertained.

1943

14 June, Oberhausen
LM329 WS/Q

Pilot Officer John Evans, twenty, son of George and Gladys Evans, of Regent's Park.

Sergeant Vincent George Louvaine Smith, twenty-eight, husband of Mary, son of George and Ethel Smith.

Sergeant Robert Borthwick, thirty-one, son of James and Mary Borthwick.

Sergeant Vincent John Tarr, second navigator.

*Sergeant Alan Wilson Waite, twenty-two, son of John and Florence Waite of Liverpool.

*Flight Sergeant Walter James Chapple, thirty-two, son of Alfred and Florence Chapple of Forest Gate.

Sergeant Herbert Ivor Ashdown, nineteen, son of Bertie and Asenath Ashdown of Cardiff.

Sergeant Derek Walter Brough, twenty, son of Frederick and Vera Brough of Dartford.

20 October, Leipzig
JB275 OF/H; No. 97 Squadron

Pilot Officer Kenneth Painter, twenty-one, son of Harry and Mary Painter of Yarnfield.

Sergeant Thomas Deacon, twenty-three, son of Richard and Rebecca Deacon of County Carlow.

(Sergeant R.C. Saunders, POW)

Sergeant James Edward Bacon, twenty-two, son of Edward and Elsie Bacon of Muswell Hill.

(Sergeant T. Andrews, POW)

Sergeant Sydney Francis Hone, twenty-four, son of George and Mabel Hone of Seasalter.

Sergeant Dennis Walter Angell, twenty, son of Walter and Eva Angell of Southampton.

23 November, Berlin
DV329 KM/W; No. 44 Squadron

Flight Sergeant Thomas Myerscough, wireless operator, twenty-two, son of James and Alice Myerscough, husband of Dorothy, of Chorley.

1944

15 February, Berlin
JB665 LE/B; No. 630 Squadron

Flight Lieutenant William English, twenty-two, son of Henry and Elsie English of Wingate.

Sergeant Norman Harold Mitchell, thirty-one, son of Samuel and Una Mitchell, husband of Hilda, of Stockport.

Flying Officer John Emlyn Evans, twenty-four, son of David and Mary Evans of Ynyshir.

Pilot Officer Llewellyn Vivian Fussell, son of Edward and Matilda Fussell, husband of Irene, of Bridgwater.

Pilot Officer Leslie George Lane, son of Daniel and Maud Lane of Wood Green.

Pilot Officer Derek Reginald Carlile, nineteen, son of Albert and Lilian Carlile of Nuthall.

Pilot Officer William Phillip Revenall Hewitt, twenty, son of William and Dorothea Hewitt of Gulgong, New South Wales.

*Pilot Officer John Leslie Richards, second pilot, twenty-eight, son of John and Beatrice Richards, husband of Mary, of Oakham.

20 February, Stuttgart
ED654 WS/W

Pilot Officer William John Chambers, twenty-three, son of Ernest and Margaret Chambers of Ilford.

Sergeant William Edward Haywood, twenty, son of William and Lily Haywood of Richmond (Surrey).

*Warrant Officer James Braithwaite Mandall, twenty-six, son of Harold and Elizabeth Mandall of Rosgill.

Technical Sergeant James John Hannon, USAAF, of Bronx, New York City.

Sergeant Illtyd Melville Mulcuck, twenty-three, son of Thomas and Bridget Mulcuck, husband of Madge, of Cilfynydd.

Sergeant Arthur Llewellyn Steward, nineteen, son of Edward and Elsie Steward of Northwold.

Flight Sergeant James John Campbell, twenty-one, son of Ian and Margaret Campbell of Naracoorte, South Australia.

15 March, Westcott
Vickers Wellington LN660/O; 11 OTU

Flying Officer James Henry Scott Lyon, DFC, twenty-one, son of James and Muriel Lyon of Sale, Victoria, husband of Margaret.

22 March, Frankfurt
LM430 WS/B

Flying Officer James White Hearn, thirty, son of Alexander and Isabella Hearn of Bonnyrigg.

Group Captain Norman Charles Pleasance, Bardney station CO, passenger.

30 March, Nürnberg
W5006 WS/X

Flying Officer James Gordon Richmond Ling, twenty-three, son of Ernest and Bella Ling of Newmins.

Sergeant Leonard Moss, nineteen, son of Edward and Minnie Moss of Manchester.

(Sergeant H. Laws, POW)

Flight Sergeant Thomas Santola Fletcher.

Sergeant Edgar Alexander Gauld, twenty-three, son of Edgar and Alexandrina Gauld of Aberdeen.

Sergeant Edward James Rush, twenty-two, son of Owen and Ellen Rush, husband of Hazel, of Calgary, Alberta.

Sergeant Italo Prada.

10 April, Tours
DV198 WS/U

Warrant Officer Colin Albert Peak, twenty-one, son of William and Rose Peak of Tursmore, South Australia.

Sergeant Eric Warnford Kindred, twenty-seven, son of Alfred and Effie Kindred of Rainworth.

Sergeant Thomas William Varey, thirty-three, son of John and Lillian Varey, husband of Doris, of Hurst.

Flying Officer John Enoch Wilkes of Barrington, Rhode Island.

Sergeant Vernon William George Torbett, twenty-one, son of William and Daisy Torbett of Hadley.

Sergeant John Weir Nelson, twenty-three, son of John and Cecilia Nelson of Lanark.

Sergeant John Hogan, twenty-two, son of Peter and Jane Hogan of Liverpool.

24 April, Munich
LM445 WS/Z

Sergeant William Bingham, twenty-two, son of Thomas and Mary Bingham of Prescot.

6 June, St Pierre-du-Mont
ND739 OF/Z; No. 97 Squadron

Flying Officer Henry William Edward Jeffery, DFM, twenty-two, son of Henry and Madeline Jeffery of Southall.

7 July, Saint-Leu-d'Esserant
JB116 WS/T

(Pilot Officer G.A. Langford, POW)

(Sergeant C.G. Fenn, POW)

Flight Sergeant John Llewellyn Wright.

(Flight Sergeant S.M. Mitchell, POW)

Sergeant Israel Feldman, twenty-two, son of Isaac and Annie Feldman of Southall.

Pilot Officer James Wright, nineteen, son of Albert and Marion Wright of Toronto.

Flying Officer Geoffrey Thomas Baseden, thirty-eight, son of Thomas and Ellen Baseden, husband of Vera, of Blackheath.

18 July, Revigny-sur-Ornain
ME833 WS/Z

Pilot Officer Leslie John Wood.

Sergeant Terence Michael Gordon.

(Flight Sergeant N. Oates, POW)

Sergeant Leslie Richard Lutwyche, twenty-one, son of Richard and May Lutwyche of Birmingham.

Sergeant David George Mumford, twenty-one, son of Frederick and Ethel Mumford of Plymouth.

Sergeant Neil Hannah.

Pilot Officer Joseph Edward Shuster, twenty-one, son of James and Sophia Shuster of Toronto.

13 August, Brest
ME757 WS/O

Flight Lieutenant Edward Harry Maxwell Relton, thirty-four, son of Edward and Edith Relton, husband of Margaret.

Sergeant Frederick Walter Johnson, twenty-three, son of Frederick and Charlotte Johnson, husband of Evelyn, of East Ham.

Flight Sergeant Charles Herbert Edwards, twenty-three, son of James and Edith Edwards of Gympie, Queensland.

Flight Sergeant John Keith Scott, twenty-one, son of John and Elsie Scott of Beechmont, Queensland.

Flight Sergeant Cyril Thomas Scott, twenty-eight, son of Cyril and Violet Scott, husband of Caroline, of Matraville, New South Wales.

Flight Sergeant Douglas William McConville, twenty-seven, son of Thomas and Alice McConville of Narrandera, New South Wales.

Flight Sergeant William Ronald Andrew, twenty-two, son of Hugh and Mary Andrew of Bell of Queensland.

23 September, Münster Aqueduct
LL901 WS/V

Flight Lieutenant Charles Berrie Scott, twenty-two, son of John and Helen Scott of Glasgow.

Sergeant Jack Edward Simkin, twenty-three, son of Charles and Mary Simkin of Seaford.

Flight Sergeant Louis Arthur Harding.

(Flight Sergeant L.W. Langley, POW)

Sergeant Maurice Edward Hayward, twenty-one, son of Maurice and Edith Hayward of Ludgershall.

Sergeant Frank Alfred Saunders, thirty, son of Andrew and Mary Saunders, husband of Ellen, of West Kensington.

Sergeant Leslie Joseph Hambly, nineteen, son of John and Ruth Hambly of Millom.

1945

1 January, Bardney
NG252 WS/R

Flying Officer Clifford Sinclair Newton, Rosewood, Michigan.

Sergeant Colin Booth, thirty-one, son of William and Ada Booth, husband of Dora, of Brighouse.

Pilot Officer Percy Grant, thirty, son of Percy and Phyllis Grant, husband of Constance, of Streatham.

(Pilot Officer R.C. Flynn, injured)

Sergeant Lawrence Gerard Kelly, twenty-three, son of Daniel and Katherine Kelly of Oldham.

Pilot Officer Edgar Harvey Cooper, twenty-one, son of Oliver and Bertha Cooper of Washago, Ontario.

Pilot Officer Robert Slade Stevens, twenty-one, son of Frank and Beatrice Stevens of Canada, husband of Margaret, of Batford (Herts).

4 January, Royan
ME300 CA/P

Flying Officer Jack Ian Coad, twenty-eight, son of Benjamin and Ada Coad, husband of Rita, of Freshwater.

Sergeant Geoffrey Arthur Taylor Boyson, twenty-one, son of George and Marjorie Boyson of Northampton.

Sergeant Joseph Charlton Dunville, twenty, son of Robert and Christiana Dunville of Hillingdon.

Flight Sergeant Harold Bert Hodder, twenty-three, son of Bert and Nancy Hodder, husband of Margaret, of Bristol.

Flight Sergeant Maxwell Browne, twenty-three, son of Eric and Vera Browne of Auburn, New South Wales.

*Sergeant Thomas Rathband Dunne, twenty-three, son of Ambrose and Margaret Dunne of Dublin.

(Sergeant R. Powell, repatriated)

12 January, Bergen
NG257 WS/N

*Flying Officer Ernest Cyril Redfern, DFC, twenty-two, son of Ernest and Rose Redfern, husband of Frances, of Salford.

Flight Sergeant John Walter Williams, twenty, son of John and Mildred Williams of Trimdon.

Sergeant Ronald William Riverston Cooper, twenty-two, son of William and Anne Cooper of Welling.

Flying Officer Owen Percy Hull.

Sergeant Lewis George Roberts, twenty-three, son of Sidney and Beatrice Roberts, husband of Lydia, of Islington.

Sergeant Walter Brand, twenty-eight, son of George and Harriet Brand of Sheffield.

Sergeant Dennis Winch, twenty, Grantham.

21 February, Gravenhorst
NG321 CA/V

Flying Officer Patrick Glenville, twenty-three, son of William and Mary Glenville of Bridlington.

Sergeant Frank Pallister, twenty, son of Matthew and Ann Pallister of Willington.

Flight Sergeant Leonard Stanley Harper, twenty-one, son of Samuel and Florence Harper of Liverpool.

*Pilot Officer Trevor John Perry.

Warrant Officer Cyril John Gallagher, twenty-two, son of James and Mary Gallagher of Oamaru, Otago.

(Flight Sergeant J.L. Nolan, POW)

Sergeant Lawrence Moore, twenty-one, son of Mr and Mrs W. Moore of Southend-on-Sea.

3 March, Ladbergen
NG325 CA/H

Flying Officer Sidney James Reid, thirty, son of Robert and Katherine Reid of Canada.

Sergeant Frank Norman Benson, thirty-three, son of John and Elizabeth Benson of Urswick, husband of Jean of Herne Hill.

Flying Officer Thomas Joseph Nelson, twenty-two, son of Frederick and Mary Nelson of Hamilton, Ontario.

Flying Officer Howard Geoffrey Harrison, twenty-one, son of Richard and Kate Harrison of Dudley.

Flight Sergeant Robert William McCormack, twenty-two, son of Robert and Eva McCormack of Liverpool.

Flight Sergeant George Frederick Caley, nineteen, son of Charles and Mildred Caley of North Bay, Ontario.

Flight Sergeant Marquis Roland Bullock, twenty-two, son of Roland and Charlotte Bullock, husband of Muriel, of Peterborough, Ontario.

7 March, Harburg
NG417 CA/P

Flight Lieutenant Frederick Joseph Abbott, thirty, son of Frank and Elizabeth Abbott of Morden, husband of Irene.

Flying Officer Hugh Henderson, forty, son of Thomas and Mary Henderson of Maghull.

Flight Sergeant James Ferguson Charlton, twenty-four, son of James and Meria Charlton, husband of Hilda, of Denton.

Flight Sergeant James Patrick Rowan.

Flight Sergeant William Ashford, twenty, son of William and Lily Ashford of Kingstanding.

Pilot Officer Jean Charles Oberneck of Belgium.

Flight Sergeant Kenneth White, son of William and Gerty White of Skegness.

Sources and Bibliography

Interviews with No. 9 Squadron airmen.

Operations Record Books and Combat Reports, Nos. 9 and 189 Squadrons.

Various records at the Public Record Office.

Commonwealth War Graves Commission.

www.aircrewremembered.com

RAF Bomber Command Losses of the Second World War, vols 1 to 6, W.R. Chorley.

The Bomber Command War Diaries, Martin Middlebrook and Chris Everitt.

The Luftwaffe War Diaries, Cajus Becker.

9 Squadron, T Mason.

Avro Lancaster: The Definitive Record, Harry Holmes.

Photographs mostly courtesy of No. 9 Squadron Archive and Terry Lintin.